A Feast of Cotswold Poems

To

Reverend Rosborough

Best Wishes

Hugh

Cotswold Poetry Series

August in Adlestrop

Camelot of the Cotswolds

Moreton Miscellany

Power Lines

Summer Lakes

The Bells of Bledington

The Campden Crown

The Evenlode Valley

The Peacock of Quenington

Venice of the Cotswolds

Windrush Winter

Animal Anthologies

The Perfect Purr - 102 cat poems

The Biggest Bark - 101 dog poems

The Royal Stallion - 100 Horse poems

A Feast of Cotswold Poems

Hugh O'Connell

BoW Books

BoW Books
7 Clapton Row
Bourton on the Water
Gloucestershire
GL54 2DN

A Feast of Cotswold Poems

Title cover by Richard O'Connell

Printed by In2digital, Ltd.,
Phoenix House, Stoke Road, Elmstone Hardwicke,
Cheltenham, Glos GL51

ISBN: 978-0-9573609-0-7

Contents

Preface

The poems have been selected from the Cotswold Poetry Series of booklets I wrote from 1994 to 2010, which covered the Cotswolds from Winchcombe in the west to Chipping Campden in the north to Lechlade in the south-east.

The background to the poems arose from my appointment to the Gloucestershire Learning Support Service. I was based in Bourton on the Water to cover primary and secondary schools in the North Cotswolds which later expanded as far as the Cirencester area and Lechlade schools

My daily travels took me through beautiful areas of the Cotswolds which stimulated an interest in the local villages. I was eager to find out more about them and accumulated a large number of local history books - a long term interest of mine with that of nature and life in the countryside.

Indeed, I have been fortunate to live in some of the most beautiful areas of Britain having being born in the Mumbles, Swansea and lived on the Gower Peninsula and later in Letchworth, North Hertfordshire and also found there a beautiful countryside.

Although it was a casual observation that triggered the first book of poems on Bourton on the Water in 1994 when my two nieces were paddling in the River Windrush under the willow tree near the first bridge in Bourton. I tried to make a painting of the scene but failed miserably. Then I wrote a poem about the scene and more ideas for poems about Bourton began to take hold. So, for each year over the next twelve years, I wrote a poetry booklet on Bourton and other booklets on North Cotswold villages.

I then began to write about villages where I felt I some connection following my regular visits to their local primary and secondary schools. The selected poems in this anthology concern the following villages: Bourton on the Water, Winchcombe, Chipping Campden, Moreton in Marsh, the Evenlode Valley and the smaller North Cotswold villages where the River Windrush flows.

Nearly all the poems in this book were a result of direct experiences from visiting a particular location and the start of many of the poems were initially written in the notebooks I took with me on my 'poetry expeditions'.

The poems are selected from eleven of the fifty booklets in the Cotswold series, and the process was guided by trying to select a range of topics and poetic forms. In the process of the selection many of the poems have been revised.

I have also tried to select poems which reflect a range of forms - free verse, stanzas, sonnets and limericks and chosen to suit a particular topic or theme, for example, the 'Chestnut Sonnets' reflecting the four seasons.

Writing can be an isolated and demanding pursuit. But when writing about a beautiful countryside such as the Cotswolds, it becomes a pleasure but also a responsibility - you want the poem to be true, accurate and vivid without over embellishment.

There poets who are 'Poets of Place' - they write about certain areas and I suppose I might come under that category. I feel very privileged to have been given the opportunity to live in the Cotswolds and few better places can there be to write about than the Cotswolds. It has a 'magic aura' and offers a visual and aural feast hence the title of the book.

I also hope the poems may encourage others to visit these villages and places and, perhaps, in turn, encourage them to write their poems.

Finally, I should also like to thank those readers and local bookshops who have supported my Cotswold poetry booklets over the past eighteen years. Their support and the beauty of the Cotswolds has spurred me to write the poems in this anthology.

Venice of the Cotswolds

What better place
To go whether young or old,
Than this village,
A Jewel in the North Cotswold.

Bourton on the Water,
Enchants sons and daughters,
As they stroll around
Different delights are found:

Droves of Ducks,
Stone roofed, rose cottages
And an ankle high river
With its five sturdy, little bridges.

Limes, beeches
And chestnuts add to the scene,
And decorate
One of the longest village greens.

A fond welcome assured
Whether its sunny, cloudy or cold,
To the timeless joys
Of 'Venice of the Cotswolds'.

Football in the River

Where else would they play football in the river
Than Bourton on the Water ?
Some say for nearly a century its been done
And its such fabulous fun !

Those early games were such a success
When players wore Fancy Dress !
Instead of shirts, socks and trousers,
They wore skirts, bonnets and blouses !

And, still, Bourton Rovers in the river play
Whenever its August Bank Holiday !
They're watched by an ever-cheering crowd,
Who laugh and shout long and loud !

But see how the crowd soon surge back,
When the players suddenly kick -
Not the ball - but the water
Over spectators who scream with laughter !

And who cares about the final score,
For nothing matters more
Than raising funds for the local team
Who, though drenched, play like a dream !

Flotilla on the Windrush

The Queen's Diamond Jubilee Celebrations, 2012

The Bank Holiday crowds gather along the Windrush,
All a quiver after Football in the River.
There's such high expectations
For the flotilla to match the Thames Celebrations !

But Bourton boatbuilders are not to be outdone
As they display home-made model ships in the sun !
The range of red and white and blue crafts
Are made from a multitude of parts -

Pop bottles, egg cartons, plastic packets, union jacks,
Tin cans, polystyrene trays and wire racks !
They've been designed, decorated and draped
And stuck together with lots and lots of sticky tape !

Some show ships with the Royal Family standing,
Others an aircraft carrier with planes landing !
And what could be more eyecatching and finer
Than the great twin funnel, red and white liner !

But the fun begins when they're launched on the water
Pursued by wading son, mother, father and daughter !
The fleet of union jack boats are gently steered
As the crowd waves flags, claps and cheers !

As cameras click and flash along the riverside edges
The flotilla bobs along and passes under the bridges !
The race to see whose in front proves a thriller -
In fact, its far superior to the Thames flotilla !

But no one really minds who wins first prize
Its the 'taking part' that really applies,
And what a grand response everyone can see
In Bourton's Flotilla for the Queen's Diamond Jubilee !

John the Hairdresser

Those bright blue eyes scan the customer
As safe as the hands that shall style his hair.
John delivers each customer's expectation
As he clips and combs raising conversation;
When a funny old world is so often put right,
With opinions vented as he combs and cut.
Greetings made, kind jokes equally gauged.
Forms hairline bonds with all his customers.
Favorites are paraded before a horse race,
But with a strict tariff limit upto twenty pence.
Humour still the best therapy ever to appear.
John's tales of day-trippers makes this clear:
The smart London man who declared John's
Trim was worth the run in his jag from Town.
Postcards from Hawaii and Spanish sands,
Photos sent by girls all the way from Japan.
The story of an old shop mirror bought and
Then restored, polished by specialist hands,
And sold to an ecstatic collector in Manhattan.
John's watercolour paintings fringe his shop
And some are bought though not for a lot.
He liked day trips such as to the Lake District
And tea dances shows he still quick of step.
Anecdotes keep alive those early days when
Apprenticed in the local cottage hospital.
Title and rank recede before the open razor,
Exposing the inner man and true character.
In the 'golden mile' note the little green shop
And a latched window ajar shows its open.
The most competitive prices in the Cotswold
And standards fit for gentlemen young or old.
Still working fit at eighty-three years young,
Forty mile round trip and home visits done.
The longest, single business still in Bourton.
And awaits John's two sons, if suitably keen,
One a barrister, the other, a university dean.

Bourton in Old Photographs

The Queen's Diamond Jubilee Exhibition 2012

Its not only the range of the photographs
but the comments of those when looking at them -

"Oh I remember my father playing football in the river.
Look forward to it all year. Loved splashing' whoever was about' !

The local blacksmith, 'took horses, as big as houses,
down that ever so narrow alley into the forge.
We'd watch him from the little window at the side.
He could fit a shoe cold. Horse loved him.
His brother was only in the army for a day,
so we called him, jokingly, the 'Colonel'.
And their sister, next door, used her sewing machine to alter
trousers to hand down as we couldn't afford new trousers.
And she'd made them a perfect fit.'

The diversity and delight of local Bourton life:
The Hunt hovering outside the Old New Inn.
Black top riding hats glistening in the sunlight.
Hundreds of spectators milling around rummaging hounds.
Building bridges, widening roads. Hartwell's smiling staff.
Doctors and vicars in big, black, shiny saloon cars.
Generations of local football and cricket teams in full kit.
Bourton men volunteering to fight in the war. Shoveling snow.
Mr Butt, the photographer on his cart in the river.
The 1952 flood. The old police station and lock-up.
The Royal Irish Rangers marching in kilted uniform.
Fetes, pageants, parades, school parties, hospital wards,
scouts' jamborees, butchers' horses and carts -
especially the photo of the horse pulling a car out of the river.

A village when everyone knew everyone
and looked after each other but also knew how to have fun.
Some believe they were the best times ever in Bourton.

Spring Conygree

Softly slip down the half-hidden, curling lane
Round the ringing of the kissing gate turnstile,
To find May time freshly up and about -
Where Bourton wears her sweetest smile
Whatever is wild and well and willingly grows
Among rambling, emerald hedgerows.

Here stays untouched, heart-held acres.
Flowers mingle like brothers and sisters -
Willowherb, buttercups and harebells.
Snowy lambs trot beside their mothers,
While others seek copper beech cover
Or leap over tufty grass, bracken and heather.

The rolling windrush parades and purrs
As a courting couple track free flowing river.
Fish hug shadows, shimmering tall firs
Guard the banks of the stone walled manor,
While the river path offers a delightful surprise,
A feast of forget-me-nots have started to rise.

Thrushes and blackbirds, no longer single,
Sing triumphantly to the blue Sunday sky.
Families on picnics settle near the river bank,
Smile at ramblers who quietly pass by
An emerald place of budding expectations,
Bristling with spring-singing conversations.

Early on Saturday morning, new tenants arrive -
A mother and nine ducklings from a home.
At first, so apprehensive they might not survive.
But instantly they start to paddle and roam,
Merrily bobbing and dipping along the river,
Bringing tears to the eyes of their deliverers.

Gilly

Sometimes people you come to love and know
Upon you, slowly but surely grow.
Such was Gilly who never let anyone down
And would always smile rather than show a frown.
She would notice when someone needed care
And for them she'd step forward to be there.
The most beloved mother and grandmother too
And her compassion to others also swiftly flew.
No matter who or what or the time of day
To help those in need she'd go out of her way.
All possible efforts Gilly astutely applied
To ensure everyone was happy and satisfied.
Deeper needs Gilly seemed to understand
And be among the first to offer a helping hand.
Gilly took so many under her wing to try
And show them how they, too, could learn to fly,
While those who with Gilly have happily sat
Loved to listen to her stories, wit and chat.
She loved her trips of which she would tell
Whether to the Races or the Dorchester Hotel.
Gilly would think about things in a special way
And make you value what was important in the day.
Her ways were warm-hearted, honest and kind,
Though ever ready to stand up and speak her mind.
Yet, Gilly never displayed a trace of self-pity
But got on with whatever the duty or responsibility.
She strove to meet whatever might be the goal.
No matter what was the task or the role -
As an Assistant Cook, Activity Helper
And for local Bourton events a steadfast supporter.
She gave to every task her whole heart
And made everyone else feel more than a part.
Perhaps, that was Gilly's greatest role
To daily share her generous, truly Christian soul;
For what is better than to help others -
Especially our less fortunate sisters and brothers,
Which was how Gilly lived her life 'giving all the time',
And for that, surely, to Heaven her good soul shall climb.

Music of Royal Courts

Medieval music from the Longsdale Consort,
Once applauded in royal courts
Of England, France, Spain, Germany and Italy.

Presented in the lunch hour
To a small audience in St Lawrence Church;
Curious to hear and watch,
Unique instruments these musicians have made -

Gemshorn, crumhorn, tabor, spinet, sordune,
Revive royal dances and melodies,
Penned by kings and distant composers.
Of the earliest, shortest forms,

One, perhaps composed by Henry the Eighth,
With a verse whose line,
"who can say mirth and play is best of all ?'
Might serve for our time.

Music connects.
Accompanied by August sunlight
In this sacred house,
Where reed and string and pipe and chord
Bring the listeners closer to the Lord.

Whatever might be music's history
It brings together the heart of the community.
And where better to gather to listen or sing
Than where church bells ring ?

Senior Advisory Teacher

She raised the learning horizons of children
In the shires and across the North Cotswolds.
Her destiny to learn, to teach, no higher gift;
Abundantly bestowed, generous and distinct.
Her expertise developed with Higher Degrees,
Acquiring mastery of specific learning difficulties
For children striving to read and spell and write,
Who achieved these skills guided by her insight.
And, surely, no better task in life worth attaining
Than to provide paths for a child to enjoy learning.
Earning and deserving her place on the summits,
Revered by her peers, her schools and parents.
Her manner and methods tactful, astute, compact.
Her love of literature, music, art were well known
And a poet whose skills were too rarely shown.
Her interests extended into things rare and old,
And postcards of her beloved Wales and the wold.
All ages welcomed her gentle humour and smile
And a sense of fun that could ease the longest mile:
Able to listen and advise, more deeply understand.
In her hand pen or pencil or chalk became a wand.
All her schools would so willingly, so happily seek
And of her skills and style would so highly speak;
As she drew upon her expertise of all resources
To match the needs of individual learning courses.
A style quietly elegant, some deemed immaculate.
Equitable to all, whatever the call, however late.
And when called far, far too soon from life's stage,
Her final moments glittered with a soldier's courage.
Here was a life that brought the stars within reach.
Yet, above all, would 'gladly lerne and gladly teche',
Children and adults in a career rising four decades;
That shall keep and glisten, and shall never fade -
For peers and pupils will always fondly remember.
Our universally admired Senior Advisory Teacher.

Brass Band on the Green

Beside the bank of the Windrush trees
Find trumpets, tubas and trombones,
Resounding across the green and lanes,
Ensuring visitors shall come back again.

Every patch of grass seems over run
On this golden-strewn August Sunday:
Grown-ups listen surrounding the green,
While children and dogs decide to play.

Melodies and film scores soon fly past
From the Cotswold's Blockley Brass Band.
Some wear peaked caps and sunglasses,
But all follow the steady beat of the baton.

Their summer performance also shows
What can prove a most memorable sight -
For encores heard on distant evenings
And waiting-in-the wings wintry nights.

War Veteran

Army No: 5184130

From a Cotswold village
He travelled over the world's ravaged stage,
Knowing his life would never be the same
Once those seven numbers had claimed his name.
Hand-written in his Regular Army booklet:
Conditions of Service in the Gloucestershire Regiment,
Dedication to duty upheld throughout the war.
An immortal decade carved a sergeant's career -
Fighting long and hard and far,
Earning medals, ribbons and the Burma Star.

Glory with the Glosters
And service with the South Wales Borderers:
Final Assessment of Conduct and Character
On Leaving the Colours: Exemplary.
But war can remain bright as gunfire in the memory
Of victors who never retire unreservedly:
Revived in recurring malaria,
Marching three hundred miles through Burma,
Manning a bren-gun at Arnhem,
To defeat what the Free World Condemned.

And though he's long been home,
He's never forgotten his comrades carved into stone,
By selling poppies to remember their memory
And planting a memorial tree in the community.
But his only commitment to new Colours
Is to favour sweet peas among all his flowers,
And moments he would treasure
Strolling down his garden path at leisure,
Or life on a lake, moments away,
With great crested grebes and herons on display.

Reach Out

We'll gladly share
The Joys of our Church,
So everyone's aware
They're here within reach.

Safe in His hands,
We'll spread His Word
Over our green lands,
Until everywhere its heard !

His Love and Light
Surpass two thousand years.
His sun brightens every night,
And takes away our fears.

And this Good News
Our hearts sing and shout,
So we'll always
Reach Out, Reach Out, Reach Out !

From the mural, 'Our Millennium Mission'
in St Lawrence Church, Bourton on the Water

Carols by the Windrush

Monday, 15 December

The East Wind howls, whistles and whines
like a wolf hunting for stray lambs.
Surely, the coldest night of the year.
The night wears a a thin black blanket.
Branches scratch and rattle windows.
Bins roll down dark lanes.

Yet, the miserly, starless sky
is soon filled by the sound of carols
sung by a crowd, drawn from warm firesides,
gathered near the Christmas tree in the Windrush,
which beams like a multi-coloured beacon,
summoning lonely ships into harbour.

The crowd comprises families young and old,
mums and dads, grandparents,
uncles and aunts, all singing together.
Sustained by laughter, hot mince pies and soup,
while Santa Claus offers presents
to bright-eyed, suddenly shy children.

The Wind Band of The Cotswold School
defies the biting wind, wrapped up in scarves
and overcoats and bobble hats.
They brave the blunt, bitter wind to hoist
their carols far beyond the shimmering river.

The whipping wind becomes their messenger,
serves to deliver their music
along the silent, running river
over and around the shadowy green,

to homes and hearts unknown,
with a message often left unsaid
the singers ring out across the village:

making everyone aware
what every carol concert declares -
they serve to remember
what is meant when falls December.

Snowdrops

Cluster of snowdrops.
Bridal white
near the gravestones.

Winter's pearl white jewels,
lighten the gloom
of shrouded, icy evenings.

January's little beacons.
Keeping small dreams alive.
Promising Spring.

The Cotswold Auctioneei

A true gentleman from the North Cotswold
With family links to the Forest of Dean and Str
And to 'The Old Manse' John's family associate
And at Dauntsey's Independent School educated.
A country boy who excelled in English and sport,
And a lifelong passion for John would prove to be
Fair play in life, cricket and especially rugby -
Four hundred and sixty one games steering low
As tight head prop for Stow Rugby Club's front row
Besides nine years as Secretary organising the show,
And with many a tale playing cricket for Bourton Vale!
He served in the RAF in the Far East and Singapore -
The keenest Drill Sergeant of the Training Corp!
Tours through France and Spain were happy times,
Sampling their cuisine and dry white wines
Or high among the glens as touring gentlemen.
But John's fate lay in the selling of land estates,
Travelling all over the North Cotswold in his career
As a highly respected valuer and agricultural auctioneer.
John, like a trusted friend, the farmers' would hail
And, when business was concluded, invited to partake
Afternoon tea - often with delicious homemade cake!
But, we must not forget John's fellow traveller,
Such as George, his favourite Jack Russell terrier,
Who happily sat on John's lap as they drove along -
When no-one was around to say it was wrong!
On auction days John's personality would fill the hall
As the bids rose which he'd acknowledge and call!
His command of the room was a sight to behold -
The finest agricultural auctioneer in the Cotswold.
And in 'The Old New Inn', if raised glasses were seen,
No one stood taller to toast Her Majesty the Queen.
Tho' his love for his family and the countryside,
Shall always fill John with the greatest of pride.

A Cotswold Carer

The Cotswold Carer post offered her a career
Which allowed her gift of empathy to appear.

In the Nursing Home she follows the ways
To care for those in their final, precious days.

She applies practical and sensitive support,
Maintaining the high standards she was taught.

She smiles and gently talks to those in her care,
And of their complex needs she's keenly aware.

She listens carefully to whoever she's near,
And helps those who feel alone, feel at home.

And finds time to converse if they're confused,
Respecting and assuring their feelings and views.

She voices concern wherever there's a need,
And thoroughly completes whatever the deed.

Yet shows a great sense of humour and fun
That eases and cheers the hearts of everyone.

While those ever closer to their lasting rest,
She comforts with words of tenderness.

Although, she'll never believe she quietly glows
Which lightens and strengthens all those she knows.

Our Kathleen

1911 - 2011

Kath was born three years before the First World War
And blessed with good health to reach five score !
A children's nanny, dressmaker and mother,
Who raised a son and daughter,
Besides beloved cats who purred around her !
Kath crochets blankets for rescue cats she adores.
Her room contains books and paintings feline,
Which she reads and smiles at all the time !
In fact, her smile is something to behold,
It welcomes everyone in from the cold.
Kath likes being busy, whatever time of day,
Whether reading the papers or doing crochet.
Far from strife she enjoys the little things in life.
Perhaps its the secret of living so long
As Kath will often say when we come along,
"Can you hear the blackbird's song ?"
Kath enjoys the seasons and the flowers,
The sunshine, the moon and even the showers.
Outside her window she watches whatever grows,
And often exclaims, "Oh, what a lovely red rose !"
And soon espies the birds flying in the skies !
Kath thrives on her regular cups of tea,
With sugars totalling, well, at least three !
Blackbirds, pigeons, cats, roses and cups of tea
Demonstrate Kath's delight in the little things,
That have given her long life its daily wings;
And a steadfast faith that shines bright as the sun,
Affirmed in once-a-month Holy Communion,
That reminds Kath of a favourite memory -
As a devoted parishioner of Tewkesbury Abbey.
Such values over ten decades has helped Kath soar
To, now, one hundred years and, surely, more !
And the most prized of all Birthday cards seen
Is Congratulations from Her Majesty, the Queen.

The Infinite Weight of a Daffodil

I saw the daffodils
swaying along the river path.

I picked one and dropped it
into my shopping bag

But, then,
the bag felt so heavy.

Like a brick
had been dropped in it.

The Perennial Temptation of The Bourton Bridge Nudge

When folk stand on little bridges
With the quite tiniest of ledges,
It's hard to resist
As you try to pass,
Quite the naughtiest of nudges!

Camelot of the Cotswolds

In dreams is it possible to revive and revere
Those legends of King Arthur and Guinevere,
Knights of the Round Table, and Merlin too,
Poetic myth and mystery believed by so few.

Until we consider what is proven and known
Of misted centuries in Winchcombe sewn.
Here were riches and royal resplendence
With kings, queens and knights in residence.

Before the advent and roar of iron machine,
When ruled the horse and plough and swords.
Before times became poor, forlorn and lean,
When ruled Kings and Chieftains and Lords.

Before storming Norman and devilish Dane,
Winchcombe christened a capital in the reign
Of Good King Kenulf and his son, Kenelm.
Regal heart and regal soul of Mercia's realm.

In later ages enjoyed by glittering Queens:
Aragon, Elizabeth; resident Katherine Parr,
Choosing eternal rest in Castle Chapel green,
First claim of all their kingdom and empire.

This gave status and fame to Winchcombe,
Where the highest and mightiest made home;
Placing their presence like jewels in the town,
Which sparkled as if Canterbury or Rome.

When Winchcombe by the world was known
As residence and home of valiant thrones,
When ruled High King and Queen and Abbot
Where the Cotswolds created its Camelot.

Sudeley Castle

In Sudeley Castle discover a detailed portrait
Depicting the history of royal courts in England,
That glistened brighter than Tuscan sunlight:
With flags and banners in steadfast hands
Deep in this evergreen, rolling Cotswold jewel;
When this castle kindled mighty monarchs -
Fledgling queens preparing for glittering reigns -
Finding rare release among its yew lined parks;
Or the three day anniversary Elizabethan feast
To celebrate the Spanish Armada's defeat.
Yet time turned tyrant and the castle crumbled,
Until its restoration and the revived story -
Echoing fabled feasts and royal applause
When Winchcombe cradled its Camelot glory.

The Legend of St Kenelm

Of all the great tales and legends of Gloucestershire
that of Saint Kenelm, son of Kenulph, King of Mercia,
is the most popular and most loved of them all.
It is a legend that can still bring to all ages a tear
For Kenelm was only seven when he took the throne.
But one of his two sisters, the vicious Quendryda,
wanted Mercia's kingdom and her brother killed.
She failed with poison and then, vixen persuader,
promised Askobert, his guardian, great title and wealth,
if her seven year old brother and liege he would kill.
But Kenelm had a dream, which he told to his nurse
while they were at Winchcombe, the Mercian capital.

Kenelm saw a beautiful tree of flowers and starry lights,
when it was cut down he flew like a dove up to heaven.
Nurse Wlwene grew afraid fearing for the child king,
but no one suspected a dreadful crime would occur
When Askobert took Kenelm hunting. The boy grew
tired and lay down to rest and sleep while his guardian
began to dig a grave. When Kenelm awoke he knew
the grave was for his body, but said that he would not
remain in the grave for he would go to a far distant place.

Then Kenelm seized an ash stick, stuck it into the ground
where it took instant root and grew into a beautiful tree.
Askobert had no mercy, he swiftly cut off Kenelm's head !
From where a dove arose and flew to the skies of heaven.
Askobert buried the corpse but a bright column of white rays
hovered above the child king's grave. A white cow, grazing
near by, came and stayed by the little grave for many days.
The pasture land grew so lush twice the milk was raised.
And the fertile land soon became famous as 'Cow Vale'.

His sister, Quendryda, seized the throne and forbid
any mention of Kenelm's name. Though filled with fear
When higher forces over Quendryda began to appear:

During mass in Rome a dove appeared by the Pope, and placed on the altar a scroll which read: 'In Clent cow pasture, under a thorn, Of head bereft lies Kenelm, king born.' To England papal ambassadors were sent !

They found the little king's grave, and when lifted with a blessing, a fountain of pure water erupted forth. When the Queen heard the good people of Gloucestershire were bringing home Kenelm's body, she raged and began to read, as a curse, the 108th psalm backwards. But when she read the lines 'Let this be the rewards of my adversaries' both her eyes dropped out, engulfing the psalter with blood ! No church would bury her, left to rot in the foulest of marshes.

Kenhelm, The Saint of Winchcombe, was gently laid to rest, next to his beloved father, Good King Kenulph. From then miracles were attributed to the blessed boy saint, especially for healing the sick and blind and beloved by all children.

For many centuries a feast of St Kenelm was held and those who dare refused were cursed with misfortune - a manor lady who denied her serfs a holiday, went blind and all her animals disappeared forever. Smiths, who worked on Sunday, found hammers and pincers stuck like glue to their hands and only prayers and penitence found them again. Though springs and wells mark St Kenelm's journey home to Winchcombe - the haven and home of saints and abbots and child kings.

This is the legend of Saint Kenelm, boy saint of Winchcombe. His miracles spread like sunlight over the hills and wolds. Pilgrims came from afar across the land to his blessed well for hope and inspiration and even to this day we still tell.

Bullet Holes in the North Aisle Wall

Here are the marks, highlighted by the sun,
From volleys of bullets by Roundhead guns.
Alleged payments to captives of the Civil War
Spent on Royalist soldiers inside church doors.
Neither trial nor plea impeded that command,
Heard so often and for so long in England -
When steel or shot would decide the final fate
Of those who fought for the sovereign or state.

The results of their sacrifices were profound,
The cruellest of any war that can be found:
When Family fights family, brother fights brother,
In the belief a civil war will never create another.
And symbolises the waste of war for one and all,
Affirmed by bullet holes in the North Aisle wall.

A Lady of Winchcombe

What is the worth of being good,
To be like Miss Anna Maria Wood ?
Born in 1782, lived within the law
And society until her death in 1864.

Devoted to her cousin; resident
In an established, well-endowed
Family home. A refined painter
Of oil portraits in perfect miniature.

With a poet's love of nature and art
And a high sense of Christian duty.
All her days she could safely chart,
Bound by high thought and beauty.

Bestowing in her will the bequest:
'warm cloaks for women and warm
stockings for men'. Dignity intact -
Stable, serene, sensible and calm.

Dr Merrett's Great Catalogue

Merited mention in Adlard's cavalcade,
Three centuries swept past since 'Pinax'
- the title of the prime catalogue of animals,
Vegetables and minerals of Great Britain.
It also contained the first list of British Birds.
Imagine the research, rigorous application,
Reference precision, the assiduous accuracy
And onus on the author - Christopher Merrett.
Honours graduate from Gloucester Hall, then
Oriel College, Oxford, followed by an M.D.
First librarian to Royal College of Physicians.
Later a group of algae named after Merrett:
Algae Merrettia - a tribute to his higher career.
The National Biography adds further details:
In 1666 the Great Fire of London destroyed
The library and states Dr Merrett's 'services
Dispensed with'; and later that Dr Merrett was
'expelled from his fellowship for non-attendance',
But held an extensive practice at Amen Corner,
Till his death at his Hatton Garden home in 1695.
This may illustrate a man of science not state.
Perhaps, a soul who discerned a chosen fate.
Full servant to his patients and natural history,
The first true bridge between nature and society.
His published works and papers issued forth:
Natural History, Medicine, Vegetable Physiology.
His pursuit of higher knowledge of great worth.
A questing mind, not the keeper of other minds.
Over three centuries ago, seeding the literature
Which spawned all textbooks and data bases,
Specialists, scholars and students now revere.
When Dr Merrett's Great Catalogue was done,
He became Natural History's 'Dr Johnson'.
And Dr Merrett's birthplace deserves merit -
Born in 1614 in the village of Winchcombe.

Mr A. Trollope

What on earth did folk think
Of a postman dressed in hunting pink ?
A passion for posting mixed with hunting
Set local postmasters and mistresses blinking !

But this pink postman was none other
Than Mr Anthony Trollope, The Author.
Who had a passion for the hound and fox
Besides claiming invention of the pillar box.

Imagine the bemused rural ladies,
Or open-mouthed Winchcombe farmers,
On seeing tramping up their paths
A huntsman carrying their cards and letters !

For Mr Trollope, so splendid in hunting dress,
Over the country was willing to tramp
To the most remote rural address,
To challenge the price of a troublesome stamp.

His target to reduce the penny surcharge
For receiving letters in rural areas and estates,
By finding, delighted as a fox, fresh short cuts
To banish the cost of extra penny postal rates.

And may even further have astonished
When the surcharge was finally abolished;
Helped by that postman in hunting pink -
Before he became an Immortal with pen and ink !

The Baritone Blacksmith

Iron mechanic for carriage, cart, buggy, coach.
The blacksmith forged the marriage of movement.
His tools held in a handled, wooden box with a pouch
of nails straight and thin, never struck bent;
a host of hammers, pincers, knives and rasps,
enough to make loitering schoolboys gasp.

Stallions, drays, ponies and mares
stood to be hoofed all without turning a hair.
But not even the older boys would dare
to shoe a horse - easier to hang on the blade of a mill.
Old shoes removed in a flash, flung on a heap.
The dipping of the new hot iron shoe,
until blue smoke sizzled and on the sole deftly placed.

Yet no horse bolted or snorted or blew,
as the hot hoof was hammered home
without a flutter in their eyes, nor a flicker on their faces.
Never a neigh, nor whinny or groan !
Despite the ringing iron mare and stallion stood quite still.
Such skills - it was waged he could shoe a horse asleep !

Other tasks were part of the Blacksmith's art:
mending iron wheels on carriage and cart,
turning iron hoops for boys to spin to and from school.
Farm worker's hoe or scythe must be mentioned.
Nothing and no-one too small for the smith's attention.

Winchcombe forge could be found in the Abbey Barn
where trader and farmer came with new and old yarns,
While the ring of hammer on anvil sang and rang,
in shadows caused by sacred cobwebs
along the row of dusty windows.

In the smithy's shop blue sparks and flames glowed
as he squeezed of the long handled, giant bellows,
which seemed to have a life of its own -
for when pressed felt like Gulliver's breath,
and embers erupted big enough to burn the town !

This Blacksmith also sang a beautiful Baritone.
In the Parish Church Choir his voice was well known
and heard singing with the ringing in his Abbey forge.

The Master of Iron and Fire of Winchcombe's World.
The Good and True Man of Our Lord and St George.

Rabbit Box House

Thirteen children filled the parents with pride,
Enough to field a rugby league side !
Although some might suggest
What else would you expect
If in Rabbit Box House you should reside ?

The Weathercock of Winchcombe

I'm the Weathercock of Winchcombe.
Over the town and hills I proudly loom.
My gilded wood as good as any gold
And I never intend to grow one day old.

I'm the Weathercock of Winchcombe.
I stand over a hundred foot tall ,
And with a tail no peacock can rival
And, next to me, eagles seem small !

I'm the Weathercock of Winchcombe.
My bright red comb is my crown.
My glittering robes by all are known
And my plumed tail has a golden tone.

I'm the Weathercock of Winchcombe.
I reign like a king over night and day.
I turn and twist and soon survey
All who come Winchcombe's way.

I'm the Weathercock of Winchcombe.
The wind and rain are my grooms.
I shed no gloom and I shed no tears
For I've been here over a hundred years.

I glisten so bright in the sunlight
And shimmer under the moon at night.
I make folk smile and lift the gloom -
The Wonderful Weathercock of Winchcombe!

Throwing In the Hat

Agreement to openly fight,
 a country sport, a pastime;
as ready as any lions
 to defend village kingdoms.
A regular, memorable sight
 on a Saturday night,
when men threw their hats
 into a ring for combat !
Bets here and there
 on a local lad's winning fists.
The match soon made -
 in shirts or bare chests.
Blows struck on fighting fields
 to cheers, roars of applause
from the gathering crowds,
 keen to keep boxing laws.
The blackened eyes,
 the kudos of bruises, injury,
blood stains on the shirt.
 Worn like laurels of victory.
In seventeenth century
 feuding village gangs met -
when Campden came
 and 'not a shirt was left'.
And legendary tales still told
 of Winchcombe winners
trouncing Tewkesbury men.
 Losers the greatest sinners.
Fighting fair, blow for blow,
 those bare-knuckled sights,
some have even hailed
 like fights betwixt knights.

Bellbones and Treacle Mary's

Of all the wondrous names in North Street
Bellbones Farm and Treacle Mary's are hard to beat:

Bellbones for what some may maintain
to be the longest and and greatest bell pull chain,
perhaps in the country, complete with horse shoe grip.
Not to mention the stirrup handle on the door
or the glistening shoe scraper with the iron lip.

And to aid access worn hand wall rails either side.
A heritage entrance full of pride.
Such a display makes modern yale lock owners dizzy
but what an advertisement for the smithy !

And if that wasn't enough
right opposite Barebones Farm lived Treacle Mary !

An immaculate home but once a sweetshop,
where Mary sold cakes and sweets;
and delicious slabs of cold rice pudding.

These most glorious names assured of local fame -
both entered in official guides
to broadcast and distribute with pride.

So, long may they be recalled by one and all -
Bellbones long bell ringing
and Treacle Mary's cold slabs of rice pudding !

Olive

Born at the birth of First Great War. One of eight children.
Her working mother would have just one slice of bread
for her lunch-time when working in the local rag house.
Dolls made from spare rags, buttons-eyes on the head.
Merry cider turned tyrant over Olive's father and family.
One of five, sometimes six, lay huddled on a double bed.
School soup tuppence and Olive had only one penny,
but not half a bowl was Olive allowed for a wintry dinner.
This often recalled as the meanest meal among many.
One mistress would dig her finger in a child's ribs or pull
back a plait hanging in front of its owner. Olive dipped her
plait in ink and when hauled back, Miss found her fingers
stained black and her face a picture of shock and anger !

After school, Olive's nightly homework was housework:
her pencil a brush, her ruler a mop, her book a bucket.
A scholar of scrubbing, washing, polishing and cleaning.
Her study a cupboard under stairs or kitchen back closet.
On leaving school, Olive rose as a dawn to dusk domestic,
learning advanced floor scrubbing ably using both hands:
wielding mop, broom and cloth graduating twice as quick,
with enough confidence to take the bus off to Cheltenham,
carrying her prized possessions in an Oxo paper bag.
Marriage dreams strengthened and forged two souls
willing to work night and day for whoever and wherever

Then Olive bought 'Bertha', a second hand bike, a symbol
of how far she had risen from her world into the real world.
Bertha never let her down as she rode across her wold
to farms and fruit gardens to struggle with stubborn sprouts,
a heavy corn sack anchored to her. Potatoes, sugar-beet,
grain, peas, Olive soldiered to pull and tug them out.
Even when mice from corn sacks suddenly ran up her leg,
Olive never screamed or danced or ran wildly about.

It was Olive's way not to complain just as it was not to beg.
Olive took her children into the summer fruit fields to pick
pears, strawberries and apples and treated it like a picnic.
Her children as fresh and ripe as the plums on the trees.
They grew into one of the healthiest and hardiest families.

Later Olive went to work in the Paper Mills, indoors at last
after years of long seasons, her fruit picking days now past;
soon preferring paper-cutting, sorting, boxing and packing
to all those barrels, crates, baskets, boxes and sackings.
Now a bus to work and canteen, all part of a happy team.
Here for Olive was the fulfillment of an unimaginable dream.

'God Is Our Inspector'

Over the entrance on the Parish Hall door,
Inscribed in Latin, the old Chapel motto,
Which should be read
And kept in the head
Of the Know-Alls: 'God is our Inspector'.

Three Jobs

During the Foot and Mouth epidemic,
a Winchcombe resident told me
about an elderly lady who lived on a farm
just outside Winchcombe.
She grew her own vegetables
and looked after a small flock of sheep.
They hardly earned any money.
So she worked part-time
as a shop assistant in Winchcombe
and ran Bed and Breakfast for tourists,
which was crucial for helping to pay bills
and get through the lean winter months.

Those three jobs gave her a living wage.
But the Foot and Mouth outbreak
discouraged tourists.
All advance bookings were cancelled.
It seemed like a plague had struck her world.
Yet, each morning, she'd drive from her farm
to the roadside, where she disinfected her boots
then changed into her 'shop shoes'.
She also started a diet to counter losses
from the outbreak.
Trying to 'soldier on', especially
when things really seemed at their darkest.

From Winchcombe to California

In the Local History section,
Locate North Cotswold texts on parade,
extended loans, respectfully worn,
including two of the 'Winchcombe Cavalcade'.

The Introduction by Massingham,
placing Winchcombe second only to Campden.
He was convinced that "a genuinely local life......
is the only life worth living".

True, then, as now, despite texts and internets.
The understanding deepened by the history
of who, why and how
in the rich, undulating loom of Winchcombe.

Another Ablard text:
'*On the Sunset Trail - A Book of California*',
which extends and expands local context.

A local life able to journey far
and produce another triumph
five thousand miles away in California.
Good stock like wine travels the world.

Endorses the power of locality. Holds its centre.
So deep, so strong. Survives oceans
and continents with confidence and style.

From Winchcombe to San Francisco
although a long, long way to go,
where better to sing Winchcombe's praises
than in Santa Barbara or San Diego ?

ADLESTROP

Down empty roads and over the little bridge
Towards things that may not be the same,
For the poet and the poem time has wedged
In what was once deepest England in a name.

ADLESTROP blazoned on the old station sign,
Matching the image long stamped in the mind;
Beside the old oak the railway seat reclines,
Coated in cream and brown its good to find:

Distant, steam-driven, piston-grinding times
When white smoke drifted over singing trees,
As trains hissed to their short halt at Adlestrop,
And one passenger turned to famously cough.

That age protected by this open station hut,
Shunting up images where its legend stood.
Now frequented by different travellers to sit
Quietly amid this flowered neighbourhood -

Combining what is both gratitude and relief,
Keeping what it could have lost - its identity:
At one with field and flower, bud and leaf.
Time only strengthens countryside purity.

And like the beauty and truth of his poetry
Grows to blossom on the heart's summit;
Still comforting travellers on their journey
To this Adlestrop they'd still opt to stop.

Adlestrop Lake

The parking area is shrouded by tall trees,
Much lower than the lake that quietly awaits
Above a shabby hut, faded notice boards,
Displaying times and dates of competitions,
For what will be prized trophies and awards
From winning eye and hand co-ordinations.
The roar from the sluice gate teems nearby
But beeches and alders offer cover supply.
The first view of the lake supplies surprises
As though from a cave the dweller emerges:

The sweep of the water, so many greens,
Fringed by even taller and grander trees
Which cast their shadows deeper, further
Over the calm canvas of the silent water.
Gnats glide and skate across green glass,
Every insect seems to relish its tiniest task.
And near the cluttered moat unfurl swathes
Of what Manet adored - sultry mats of lilies.
Such whiteness could compete with snow
And shadows seem to brighten their glow.

Around the edge of the pond anglers wait
Tracking fish that will twist and turn too late.
But now only two fishermen, father and son,
Prepare to concoct a battle plan of action -
Selecting the hooks and bait for their rods,
Serenaded by hidden finches and blackbirds.
A rummaging rook circles the languid lake
As a scuttling squirrel makes branches shake.
But the green cloth of the water will not slip,
Unless from its hidden world a fish is ripped.

Pondskaters

Lake riders often play hide and seek
In the shadows of the beech -

Where pondskaters slide and spin
For their legs are long and razor thin.

They dart and jump almost together
As if its easy skimming water !

But, no doubt, adhere to a strict diet
For the danger of too much weight

Would cause them to sink
Beneath their trusted, shimmering rink,

Where waiting torpedo fishes
Pray for pondskaters to dive on crutches.

And though we might try
We could never equally skate or fly -

Is there nothing really, really any better
Than the furious fast-forward life of a pondskater ?

Though we might be amazed
It would only drive us into a daze,

To stumble, stagger and slip off their glittering rink,
And into those cold, dark, fatal depths sink.

Miss J. Austin

Some might have observed even her luggage,
Like its passenger, never lowered the carriage.
Reflecting disposition and status of the owner:
Discreet, self-assured, ever a dutiful daughter.
Astutely aware of her rank in a civilised society,
Seamlessly blending into conduct at a Rectory.

How she might have wandered in Adlestrop Park
And thoughts sown would to a world later appear,
Providing such pleasure far beyond her lake walk.
Such delights compressed in her too brief years.
Her deeper feelings found weaved within words
That mirrored her isolated and refined standards.

Nor confined to depicting dreams of the manor,
Or an engagement with a dashing young owner
When wandering the paths along the Evenlode.
She escaped the confines of the spinster's role.
A gifted witness of a society she re-constructed
In characters of feminine single status created.

And those quiet eyes were also swift to detect
Complex relationships found in a family house,
Which few others would rarely sense or suspect,
But as a literary lioness often playing the mouse,
She saw the hawk and dove in the human heart
And in her heroines and heroes memorably chart.

Black Horse

In the paddock he quietly grazes,
  Ignores passing glimpses and gazes.
Then rubs the grass against his back.
  His belly exposed to a rain attack.

He seems to be reaping secret stores
  Far from campaigns in racing wars;
Back with whom he trusts and knows:
  Blackbirds, cows, horses, swallows.

His black coat shimmers dark and bright
  Like some blanket slipped off moonlight.
The only discontent from flies who rail,
  Though casually swept aside by his tail.

Then he ambles slowly over the grass,
  Quite determined not to let one cud pass.
Suddenly half-turns his head to one side,
  Hearing another horse taken for a ride.

Something makes him rise and rear.
  He waves his tail and cocks both ears -
A sudden beating of hooves on the grass,
  Rouses feelings when he races fast !

He keeps his head high, alert and still,
  Looks at tracks and trails up the hill;
Sensing he'll soon be taken far up there,
  Training for trophies only a few dare.

Peasewell Wood

This high wood courted their community
Which village folk shared with the gentry,
When everyone called this their Camelot
Serving Saints Days or to a tennis match.
Here harmony was always found at home
Cresting their low world of soil and stone,
And flanked by brazen beauty to this day
For such joys have never withered away.

And deep within these woods filter paths
Where rising leaves carpet shaded earth,
Overcast by sycamores, ashes, beeches
Who weave worn, bare, buckled branches
Like souvenirs from far-off, magic dances.
This wood also values, urges differences
Whose leaves offer simple, tender lessons
Laden in colours coated by the seasons.

Curling tracks riddle these singing woods
Still guiding their way to unrivalled goods.
And what better sets for summer stages:
Peeping yellow fields among tall hedges;
Sunlight lapping trunks like long bangles;
Speckled wonders down dells and dingles;
Shrouded birds singing late into the night
Funding further days of unbridled delight.

But here in the emerald heart of the wood
Pumps a deeper, darker, daunting blood,
That tracks every footfall like some prey
And only halts when such steps go away.
Yet who could wish for richer company
For beauty deepens wedded to mystery,
Found within a wood that amply survives
And when seen and sensed sharpens lives.

Dead Mole

Below the laurel bush the mole reclines.
Death turned him on his right side.
His coat has become a furious feast for flies.
Insects hurry there to seed and reside.

Turning him by foot is as close as I want to get.
His shrivelled eyes permit no gleam.
Beak, fang or poison scuttled their target.
No longer will this mole root for his team.

His tiny pink claws have ceased to tear
The soil to make a tunnel here. The flies
Re-group to attack again. Nature sheds no tears.
A tiny death under the bluest of summer skies.

But something like this should not be passed.
Dignity and respect is needed at the last.
So a handful of grass and a few laurel leaves
Over the palm-size corpse are gently cast.

Though this mole is now long past
No-one will mourn his absence from the lawn.
For every time he made a mound
Gardeners were desperate to run him down.

But that does not ease this slightest of deaths
That shall soon dissolve back into earth.
Though, surely, we should consider death
To help evaluate the purpose of our breath.

The Phantom Footprints

Long ago, when Adlestrop had a primary school
The Secretary felt a distinct and bitter chill,
As when she looked around the room
She saw what struck her with a feeling of doom -

For there on the carpet was imbedded
Two footprints that she, at once, dreaded !
She stared and gulped and left her station
Hoping the Headteacher could offer an explanation !

But not even he could find any reason
For explaining the footsteps that compelled attention.
The Secretary later called at the Post Office
To post the mail and ask for further advice !

There she was told that once in Adlestrop Hall
A half-glimpsed ghost would sometimes call
Shortly after the Butler took his life !
Perhaps, the footprints signalled ghostly strife !

And when the Secretary was asked
Where she was placed to perform her tasks,
The answer to the phantom footprint mystery
Seemed resolved as she worked in the old Pantry !

Yet nothing applied could erase the footprints
Which lasted for a month, but then they suddenly went
As quickly as they had first arrived -
Which left staff and children even more mystified !

Though, surely, it seems the proper thing
For a lovely Cotswold village to possess a Haunting ?
And what could sound any better
Than 'The Phantom Footprints of the Butler ' !

The Bells of Bledington

How the bells ring on Christmas Sunday !
So those who live far away
Can join and celebrate
The Birth that opened Heaven's Gate !

For the Bells of Bledington
Ring the praises of His Son.

Listen to each and every bell,
As together they tell
The carols we sing this morning
Herald the glory of Christmas dawning !

For when the Bells of Bledington peal
No greater hope can we feel !

Here the bells bring the joy
We always find in that baby boy,
Far, far beyond the village green
To homes and hearts unseen.

So Bells of Bledington ring again,
Raise the Spirit in Everyone !

For every chime and peal
Echoes what we feel,
Over trees and roofs, fields and skies
What His son always supplies !

And Bells of Bledington ring most of all
When our hearts hear silence call !

So Bells of Bledington ring again and again,
Awaken the spirit and soul in everyone.
Here on Christmas Day
And with us always stay whether near or far away !

'Life Among the English'

The title on the book stall
seems to say it all -
their enjoyment of a village fete
where no-one minds if you arrive a little late;
or offers politely made
for what is so carefully displayed.
Where smiles are many
within such comfortable, controlled company -
children quietly queue for a slide or two,
while gran and grandad retire
for a cake and another cup of tea.
And those who help do all sorts of things
from baking cakes to selling ear-rings;
washing-up or looking after a baby;
they do everything so very ably.
And the gentlemen who seem so assured
in the role of stall holder or steward,
while vicar and doctor and councillor
chat everytime they gather and hover.
For the summer fete invariably binds
their village to raise more church funds,
so they can keep what has gone on
for so very, very long
and, in the traditional way,
what crystallizes this very day,
is the village itself being justly celebrated -
as though a prize cake decorated
on a late August Saturday afternoon,
which will end very soon.
But so very, very rewarding they all agree,
and then, invariably, decide its high time
for a well-deserved fresh pot of tea.

'Life Among the English' by Rose Macaulay
(William Collins of London, 1942).
Bledington Fete Book Stall, 1998

Bledington Fete Games

Skittles, Roller-a-disk, Cork Fishing,
Squirting Dinosaur and Elephant,
Rollerball, Under the Pig, Aunt Sally,
Tiger's Bouncy Castle, Coconut Shy,
What's Under My Chimney ? Jousting,
Card for a Bottle, Don't Ring the Bell,
Bash the Rat, Bledington Balloons.

If You Don't Mind Water In The Face,
Falling Over, Getting Soaked in Public,
Trying to Hit Really UnhittableThings,
Gloating Strangers Watching You Die,
Throwing Hoops Far Too Small To
Slip Down a Fat Stick. And, of course,
Losing Again and Again and Again !
O, But what a Smile when You Win !

Breaking Tea Records

At the entrance - and still available - numbered
photographs of events to raise funds to restore
the church bells. Inside the bold lettering of
'The Local History Society', above a hanging wooden
cabinet containing 1908 china of the Chapel Anniversary
of the Wesleyan Missionary - two white plates, cup and
saucer and plate, and a white jug. Three blue tickets
refer to a Mask Ball. But, even then, numbers obviously
felt to be of especial significance, for scribed in ink,
the champion statistic is declared: '120 for tea !'

Today, ninety years on, its a hot August afternoon
that hosts the 1998 Village Fete. The announcer urges
the growing crowds to go inside the Village Hall
and 'Relax with a cup of tea'. In the kitchen, seven women
ensure everything is properly served - cutlery wrapped
in tissues for 'fresh ploughmans', assorted cakes
and tea poured into bright white cups and saucers.
A bowl of cream regularly whipped. Tongs used every time
when strawberries are plucked from an ice-cool bowl.
Ladies of the Church so pleased to see plates wiped clean.

Windows opened to bring the breeze in.
The clatter of cups and plates and the running of taps
punctuates requests and deserts topped up by smiles.
Bulging carrier bags, plants, bric-a-brac placed on
the stage. Tea keenly sipped. The cool hall brings relief.
Older folk sit with young families coming and going
between buys and rides. Cakes for sale soon sold out.
Friends show off what they've bought.
Though still early afternoon, 120 for tea easily beaten.
A result the former champions would have welcomed.

The Lovers of Bledington Orchards

Emma was the daughter of a gentleman farmer
And Daniel the manservant of the manor,
But station and class for those below or above
Could not halt the path of true love.

Although her father was against the match -
For he did not believe Daniel a worthy catch,
The manservant and the farmer's daughter
Knew they were destined for each other.

Against all the rules and codes of their time
They dared to break the unwritten crime -
All for love risked fierce adversity
As they vaulted the barriers of society !

At midnight they left the house without raising alarm
And took the road towards Cheltenham.
And to show she would never turn back,
Emma gave Daniel her gold chain and watch.

Emma never wore that gold watch again -
To show a lady's life she had abandoned all claim.
And a few hours after leaving the stage
Daniel and Emma had taken vows of marriage.

Emma's father was so outraged he charged
Daniel for deserting his station and docked his wage.
So their wedded bliss was soon curtailed
When Daniel was imprisoned in Oxford Jail !

Their love caused bitter family strife
Besides open rejection by 'higher society life',
But true love proved far deeper
And far stronger than her father's anger.

Emma pined and Emma wept,
And as for Daniel not one night slept;
For neither could understand
Why anyone should want their love banned.

Emma was asked and Emma was given
Offers to abandon her husband to prison,
But what they said only led Emma
To cry she was first a wife then a daughter !

Finally she took her decision
That shook the walls of Oxford prison -
For nothing anyone did
Could persuade Emma to take any food !

Her days and the nights eased with water
But despair soon engulfed her father,
When he saw Death awaited his daughter
And his decision would cause her slaughter.

Though Emma's family could not endure
What she believed to be love so pure,
To ensure her survival
They requested Daniel's release from jail.

Within hours of Daniel returning to Emma
She soon began to grow stronger,
Like the sun escaping from a cloud
And so they lived together happy and proud.

And though their story is long past
Who has heard of such a noble fast ?
They deserve Cupid's awards -
The Lovers of Bledington Orchards !

Barn Conversion

I remember rough boards hid the windows
And others criss-crossed barred the doors.
Holes ruled the roof and cracks gable walls.
Each day the old barn looked about to fall.
And greedy grass swiftly crept ever further,
Over paths as though their natural owner.

Then, one day, appeared the SOLD sign -
And vague prospects loomed of renovation.
Then came ladders, mixers, a gravel lorry
Arriving like some builders' rescue cavalry.
To them, damp and rot were hardly trouble,
Just chucked into skips like any other rubble.

The whistling roofers seemed to make magic,
For the puckered roof disappeared so quick.
New beams made it look an upside-down ship.
Launching, again, the old house on a new trip.
Tiers of floor planks glistened before the sun,
Soon shielded by Cotswold coloured stones.

For a week empty windows looked windswept:
Great, black, gaping, square caves at night.
Then came the stars of the re-vamped show -
Huge sheets of dark glass for the front window.
Reflecting a style beyond that of ordinary glass,
Raising the old barn into a far superior class:

The roof now glows under the dark grey slates;
Walls now bristle restored to their prime states;
The oak front door now gleams even in the rain;
As if some weed has become a sheath of grain,
Or some ugly duckling, abandoned and alone,
Is now transformed into a swan of a barn home.

Chipping Campden High Street

The Most Beautiful Village Street in England,'
Declared G. K. Treveleyan, the great historian.
A High Street praised by poets and laureates,
On canvas and etchings by royal academicians.

For the centuries still stir in Campden's heart,
Cultivated in the splendour of the High Street;
Where once cattle and sheep, horses and carts,
Filled its precincts from every corner and part.

The High Street displays a golden necklace
Of slender curves, studded with stone gems;
Still shimmering and reflecting royal reigns,
From fourteenth to the twentieth century.

Gables sundials and brimming chimneys,
Greville's House, so naturally weathered.
Its intricate dormers and mullioned windows,
And steep roofs angled like playing cards.

Elizabethan courtyards superbly portrayed
With pointed, shaded, deep-set doorways;
Gargoyles, pumps, tubs, barrels displayed
And hanging baskets of flowers arrayed.

The fourteenth century houses and inns,
Beside the fifteenth century grammar school
Buildings that have been built to befriend,
Around the principal star of the Market Hall.

The Woodstaplers' Hall beckons one and all,
Home of the mighty wool merchants of England.
And, not forgetting, the power of the Town Hall,
Presiding over this street of stone carved jewels.

ii

Yet the claim of the High Street signifies
The harmony between its ranging styles,
As though there was some divine design
To hold the ages and transcend the miles.
Not by parchment, picture, word or dream,
But the placement of stone by master hands:
To construct homes to peacefully, happily live,
And serve to inspire those from distant lands.

Harmonious hotels display their five stars,
Though distant centuries remain golden,
And, within, we freely roam near or afar,
Before wonders of the Campden throne.
When the unity of art and life both combine,
To serve as a lasting memory for all time.

iii

A High Street worthy of Master Masons.
A High Street worthy of Golden Gowns.
A High Street worthy of Mighty Merchants.
A High Street worthy of the Cotswold Crown.

A High Street worthy of an Horation Ode.
A High Street worthy of the Highest Name.
A High Street worthy of the Artist and Poet.
A High Street worthy of the Cotswold Crown.

A High Street worthy of Homage and Honour.
A High Street worthy of Apollo and Venus.
A High Street worthy of Chipping Campden.
A High Street worthy of the Cotswold Crown

The Wool Merchant's Daughter

Wool merchants offered their riches
To build the great 'Wool' Churches;
But would this merchant have preferred
Poverty than lose his youngest daughter ?
How can gold replace a beloved child ?
She died of poisoning, pricking a finger
When colouring silks. Her beauty caught
In a small mural by an Italian sculptor,
Which illuminates her gracious nature;
And more the pity at her swift departure.
Her delicate hands exquisitely carved
Forever flawless and by age unmarred.
And their daughter shall never grow old,
Her beauty safe in stone in the high wold.

The Antiquarian

A rare Antiquary of Campden called George Ballard,
Of good family but poor parents, and though devoted,
Lost his father when only three causing great hardship.
His mother took to midwifery to support seven children.
Delicate health kept him from plough and shears.
He loved collecting coins and apprenticed at a stay
To be a habit maker. Though from a humble home,
He loved words and met the challenge to learn Latin
And sought entry into the exclusive scholar's world.
He wrote out by hand the Anglo Saxon Dictionary,
Also adding one thousand contemporary words.
He visited London and Oxford on foot. He found
Sponsors among the local gentry - and gained
A place at Oxford University, and, there, became
An acknowledged authority on Erudite and most
Esteemed subjects: the Anglo Saxon Language
And Numismatics. He was admired by nobles
And wrote a history of Campden Church in 1831.
Over forty years later it was read and admired
At The Society for Antiquarians and provided a basis
For subsequent accounts of Cotswold Churches.
He defended Church monuments from destruction
And also demonstrated he was a pro-feminist.
He published in 1752 *Memoirs of Learned Ladies*
Holding sixty two descriptions of women celebrated
'for their writings or skill in the learned languages,
of arts and sciences'. He emulated Chaucer's Clerk
And matriculated at forty four years of age and elected
A Scholar clerk of Magdalen and Beadle at Oxford.
He took study and rooms for five years. He fulfilled
Half a century of rigorous study and rare scholarship.
His Works and Research comprise forty four volumes
Of Letters and Papers placed in the Bodleian Library.
He was take ill with the stone and returned home
To Chipping Campden where he died in June, 1755.

A poor and sickly lad who, by study, won a place
At Oxford University. Devoted scholar and gentleman
Of high principle and moral decency. He retained
A lifelong reverence for his mother and father.
Surely, a worthy Campdonian of his day and the ages.

The Campden Crown

Driving down Conduit Hill the heart begins to fill,
As Chipping Campden glistens, who can resist her ?

Surely, the El Dorado of the North Cotswolds !
Her glories well-known, created in golden stone.

Village of the sun and master masons of the ages.
Her prized heritage found in mansions and cottages.

She's surrounded by her wold of yellow and green,
While adorned in gold wearing her Cotswold crown.

Scuttlebrook Wake Pageant

The town crier leads the pageant in a purple coat,
And rings a bell along the High Street to one and all !
Here comes the new queen on her garlanded boat.
She waves at the crowd and children on high walls.

In the square, the Fool of the Morris Men exceeds
All expectations, as he masterly directs operations.
His dress and colours would outrival a harlequin
And he wins from the crowd instant admiration.

Campden Morris Men are forever united together,
Sing and dance whatever might be the weather.
The transfer of regal power outlined in rhyming verse,
Which the new queen affirms as though its her first !

Her wishes to champion what hath memorably past,
Should continue with more dance, games and revelry;
For the Way of the Wake is to bring and share delight,
Across Campden from Westington to the Conygree.

In costumes and dress they keep alive the spirit of joy,
Fast held by generations of families and friends;
Whether serving as dancers, pages, queens, kings
And visitors who will fondly remember such things !

For its supporters, from near and far, all understand -
Scuttlebrook Wake is the Spirit of Village England !

The Olimpick Torchlight Procession

There is no brighter festive Cotswold sight
Than Dover's procession of Olimpick torchlight !
Down Dover's Hill cascade a river of beacons,
Held by friends, visitors and citizens of Campden !
Dover's glistening army, lights up Cotsall land,
When the procession starts marching, marching !

The summer evening filled with friendly flames,
To herald the fiery finale of the Cotswold Games !
Plumed Dover leads his glittering command -
To follow horse and pipes with raised red lights.
Silvery stars support the shimmering procession
For the most stunning of Cotswold's night sights !

Whether to the centre, to the left or to the right,
A feast of flames flow and bring devilish delight !
They march into Campden down Dyer's Lane,
Carrying their torches of flickering flames !
A flame parade like no other will ever be seen,
For its the Spirit of Dover's Olimpick Games !

No matter how long the procession will last,
Residents smile as the red army flows past!
When Dover's games were famed over England
They inspired the pens of Drayton and Jonson;
Kept alight by what the marchers now command,
Descent into Campden for a joyful Celebration.

What happier Cotswold sight so embracing,
Than Dover's midnight army a-dancing, a-dancing !
And the joy and delight of sport and pleasure,
Finds the countryside's highest expression
On Dover's Hill, where its beloved and treasured -
Crowned by the Olimpick Torchlight Procession !

Field and Arena Events

a canon fires its shot
and the Olimpick games are opened on the spot:

the sack race proves a mighty trek,
when competitors are tied and bound upto the neck

spurning the bar requires hard labour -
a cotswold version of throwing the caber

cavaliers from royalist fables
fight duels with wooden sabres

shunting a plank wins lots of laughter
and running with one leg tied to a panting partner

for the five mile race you need to be in shape,
though the crowd clap those past the castle gate

the Morris Dancers jump and jingle,
cause hearts to leap in girls married or single

kicking your rival's shins can really hurt -
no matter how much padding you insert !

a funfair with rides and coconut stalls,
a space twister and bouncing balls

but the alsatian dog team and bucking bronco
almost steal the summer evening show

until the air balloon rises high into the night sky,
where the night owls and bats fly

as stewards nurture the beacon's flames
to celebrate Dover's Annual Olimpick Games !

The World's First Steamboat Inventor

He became a yeoman farmer
But Jonathan Hulls was quite fantastic !
A pupil of Chipping Campden Grammar
And a 'born lover of mathematics'.

Jonathan showed a scientific mind,
And was forever driven to find
A method to power a sailing boat.
Yet needed no wind to stay afloat !

In 1737 Hulls pamphlet appeared,
Describing the world's first steamboat,
And from a patron in Moreton
He received vital financial support.

Hulls boat was duly launched on
The River Avon in Evesham.
Would it succeed or would it fail,
The world's first boat without a sail ?

The 'boat' looked rather odd -
An axle hooked to a crankshaft,
Which turned six rear paddles
To propel the first ever mastless craft.

But the boat only shook, then fell apart
And slowly sank into the river !
And so did Jonathan's great invention,
Amid a vale of scorn and derision !

Yet Hulls made other inventions -
A slide rule to gauge malt
And an instrument to identify fake gold,
But his steamboat lies long forgotten !

Old Dolphin

The jobs of Old Dolphin -
Poet, pensioner and postman.

He wore flowers in his hat
And loved to stop and chat.

When Old Dolphin grew older,
He carried a kitten on his shoulder.

Whatever weather - sun, rain, gale, snow,
To deliver the Royal Mail Old Dolphin would go.

He wore his crown of flowers,
When he delivered cards and letters.

And wrote verses for everyone.
Sometimes serious and sometimes for fun.

So let's praise and raise
a Toastie to the Postie -

To that most delightful man -
Dear Old Dolphin of Campden !

The Conservationist

L.S. Griggs (1876 - 1938)

At the start of the new century he arrived on his tricycle to stay
In a village that seemed to suit His dreams and temperament -
And with a heart sufficient to win all those he greeted in Campden.
He soon furnished Dover's House with what was deemed the best.
But, in time, country life and ways usurped choices of earlier days -
Silver candlesticks, fine antiques replaced by iron plates, raw oaks.
He grew to love English rural life, even during hardship and strife.
Its seasons, festivals, harvests. His pictures, real and imaginary,
Seem dreams from a fairy story. Yet also contain darker shades,
Aware that it might soon all fade. He preferred the steady company
Of craftsmen to the artistic society. His friends found among furniture
Makers, upholsterers and carvers. Sharing that much deeper delight
In what hand and eye can create. Draughtsman, topographical artist,
Campden's first environmentalist. Yet still those drawings, etchings,
Cards, sketches, prints, paintings convey an impression of weight,
Whether by pen, pencil or paint from roaming over the Cotswold.
A born master artist among stone that matched the master mason.
Though a convert to the Catholic Faith, his true temporal mission,
Found by keeping another 'faith' in the conservation of Campden.
He valued Campden's architecture, weathered by time and nature;
Perceived more than for pleasure, defended when and wherever -
The Crown Jewels of Cotswold Treasure. And not only for them,
But after winning the final vote in favour of his design of Campden's
War Memorial, he placed his ruby among the High Street diamonds.
Further commissions duly staged across a host of Cotswold villages.
The Camden Trust also declared standards would be maintained -
Phone cables placed underground and would remain safe and sound.
He served for over three decades, ensuring Campden did not fade.
His gas lanterns cast such a light, house designs dazzled at night.
He risked his health and wealth to seek out, save and secure -
Dover's Hill; wrought iron signs; grey telephone boxes; local stone
To build and blend council homes; Campden House and, also from
The United States, the Market Hall. His beliefs and testament aptly
carved across Dover's House - The First Cotswold Conservationist.

The Campden Dancer

Now who could equally compete
   With the Master of Campden Dancers,
And merrily perform in the High Street ?
   Matching skills found in football as well,
A winning member of the town's Excels.
   He'd never read a line of Shakespeare,
Yet his sweet songs could bring a tear.
   His spellbinding tales would bring
Children from play to gather around him:
   To the village he brought joy and fun,
As their prized singer and story teller.
   His talents shone as bright as the sun.
He took his dances to the war as well,
   But within a year fell in the Dardanelles.

The Man who Stopped the King

Can you imagine the celebrations ?
How the church bells rang !
When, in 1908, Edward the King,
Arrived in Chipping Campden !

Flags and bunting everywhere,
As crowds of loyal folk,
Cheered their greetings,
Like hearts hewn from royal oak !

Then, from out of the crowd,
Ran a man carrying a bag !
He stood in front of the royal car,
Waving a newspaper like a flag !

The crowd seemed to freeze.
What was the reason for his action
Police rushed forward to seize the culprit,
About to ruin the Royal celebration !

But Bob Dickenson was trying to sell
The local newspaper to the King,
Who accepted it extremely well,
As if an everyday sort of thing !

After that momentous occasion,
Bob carried the 'King' on his back,
Via a picture of the Royal Crest,
Stitched across his newspaper sack !

Chinese Wilson

Among an array of delicate leaves
below the tower of St James' Church,
the colours of beauty are allowed full sway
in a garden of rare flowers, tree, shrubs and plants.

First found by a young man,
born in the heart of Campden,
who rose to become 'Chinese' Wilson, a botany legend.

Family roots registered in seventeenth century Campden.
Ernest Henry, the seventh son, born in 1876 in Lower High Street.

Apprenticed as a nurseryman
and leading down destiny's path to Kew Gardens;
revealing a fascination for flowers and plants,
herbs and shrubs, which, in 1899, took Wilson to China,
and, after many adventures, he found what might called
the Holy Grail of Ornamental Trees -
The Dove or Handkerchief Tree.

He also introduced a new fruit to Britain,
which was called 'Wilson's Chinese Gooseberry',
and when later planted in New Zealand, named, 'Kiwi' Fruit.

The finger of destiny turned oriental green.
He acquired the nickname, 'Chinese' Wilson
after leading many flora expeditions to South East Asia:

China, Japan, Bolin Island, Formosa, Korea, Tasmania,
Australia, New Zealand.

He penetrated almost impenetrable jungle,
crossed deep swamps and scaled perilous mountains,
and was constantly besieged by insects,
and the threat of fatal, untreatable diseases.

His dogs accompanied him as his loyal companions.
He also won the loyalty of his teams,
who returned to work for him again and again.

An untreated injury to his leg while hunting for the regal lily,
caused what he described as his 'lily limp'.

*Wilson introduced some 1200 species of trees and shrubs,
and collected over 100,000 herbarium species.*

He received a doctorate and prestigious awards,
rising to Director and Keeper of the Arnold Arboretum
at Harvard University.
Then, a one autumn day in America,
when he was driving his car with his wife,
they fatally skidded on wet leaves.

He was only fifty four years of age.

In 1984, the Ernest Wilson Memorial Garden
was opened at Chipping Campden,
where a host of his most popular and admired shrubs
and plants are nurtured including:

*Lilium regale, the Beauty Bush, anemone,
the Paperback Maple, rosa clematis.*

And, the Holy Grail of Plants, once of China,
now at home in the Cotswold heart
of Chinese Wilson's Memorial Garden -
The Handkerchief Tree.

The tree from China, once as rare as its discoverer -
Master of the Oriental Garden
and a Great Botanist of the World.

A Champion of Campden

This Columbus of the Cotswolds,
Prose shepherd favouring the fold
With a style to match natural verse,
Inspired by Campden's countryside.
He arrived alone in the early thirties
And resided in a rented hill cottage
With his devoted dog, Whiskey.
They strolled along lanes and fields
Around Campden and Saintbury.
Climbing over dry walls at dawn,
Until they fell into the golden arms
Of their beloved Chipping Campden.
He recorded every month that year
Of things others had so rarely seen.
He sensed heavenly behaviour,
When he saw the Cotswold green;
Snowfalls over dells and combes;
Songs of blackbirds and thrushes;
Dew laden dawns, long sunsets
Across glorious, flowering grasses;
Rustling flight of hedgerow wrens;
Swifts; blackcaps; shy turtle doves;
Woodcreepers; jousting jackdaws
Skirting lonely, forgotten waysides.
Christened a 'Chaucerian motley'.
Every wild flower was a beauty -
Rising rosebay willow herb, tansies,
Pink yarrow, sweet viper's bugloss,
St John's wort, centaurea, poppies,
Above all, 'queenly corn marigold'.
He noted flowers, birds, dawns,
Animals and local 'Yawnie' yarns.
Wrote pen-portraits of local legends -
Jimmy Teapot and "Slap" Brakeman.
He relished rural feasts in taverns:
The Bakers Arms, The Nine Bells,
The Red Lion and The Volunteers.

Befriended furrowed, farming men.
The wintry log fires warmed his pen.
And no-where else could match
The Companionship of Campden -
Though his love of leaf and glade
Could not deter or help grief fade,
When Whiskey breathed no more.
He, then, began to note and store,
His ears attuned to listen to the burr
Of high, golden Gloucestershire.
Savouring riches of Cotsal phrasing
Rivulets from Shakespeare's ocean:
"A Cotswold sentence has a hill in
its midst and curved as the country'.
Homely phrases from the cowman
Of falling rain 'on the winder like a lot
of sausages a-smackeling in the pan".
He toured Coln; Bourton; Withington;
Chedworth; favoured Winchcombe;
'Pleased with many-gabled Stanton'.
Always alert, aware, attuned, astute
To sense the spirit across the wolds,
In stones, barns, barrows or woods.
From glories of the 'wool' churches
To those little churches like Hayles;
Or the wall-paintings in Oddington.
All served to weave a Cotsal canvas.
No other has equalled or surpassed.
He reflected on the high, north wold,
Where he believed he had carved
Within, 'a larger, deeper, saner Self';
Being the 'only desirable immortality' -
Discovered and permanently upheld
By this Champion of the Cotswolds.

H. V. Massingham - 'Wold Without End' (1932)

Jimmy Teapot

He was called, "Teapot", after his uncle,
Who he helped to pick stones off roads.
Jimmy Teapot tales would always tickle -
Drank his tea from the spout of a kettle.
Hired to scare birds from the cherries,
Used claps, rattles, booming curses.
Cudgel in his right hand ready to strike,
While his left hand pulled a tin sheet.
Cherry Scarer, performed by a cripple,
And a past master of the daily tipple.
Jimmy's acting in the knighthood class,
Able to halt any visitor who might pass,
By crawling in pain across the street,
As if too weak to be able to use his feet.
When coppers placed into Jimmy's hand
He blessed whoever - then, Lo, did stand !
Teapot's opinion sought on touring radio,
Which visited Campden in the Forties.
Asked who he would most like to be like,
He replied, 'What's 'is name, up in London,
the man as smokes cigars'. And, then,
Sent a box of King Edward cigars in post !
Jimmy's joy was brew and grub roast !
Breakfast might consist of a rabbit whole,
Two sheepheads with spuds and onions.
At the Baker's Arms, Jimmy would order
Half dozen raw eggs which he'd gently
Break on his scrumpy mug rim, and pour
Into the golden liquid; and, then, casually
Consume, without drawing breath, in one
Smooth, silent and totally stunning action.
A further cry for his usual quarter of loaf
And axe-shaped slab of cheddar, settling
Down to finally devour, 'summat to yut'.
Yet, not always greedy, proved when called
To his bedroom window to devour surplus
Piglets but rejected for being far too small !

The Galloping Hairpin

The Vicar's wife was very well known,
Over six feet tall and beanpole thin.
In drab grey she'd dress,
And everywhere rushed,
Thus christened the Galloping Hairpin !

Old Flo

The cockney who'd come
From good family in London,
But was a Dickens of a sight:
Her front door always open
And by the coal fire she'd sit,
Puffing away on a clay pipe.
Sought pub snugs everyday
And ordered stout takeaways.
She'd often try to borrow
A half-crown off neighbours;
Or tap on next door's window
To ask to play on their piano,
A few songs from long ago.

Scuttlebrook Sprinter

Chippy will never forget her name -
The Perfectly Peerless Polly Wain,
Doyen of the Alms House Dames !
At ninety years gained fame,
When she ran in the Scuttlebrook Games !

Market Hall

In a village some call 'the Stairway to Heaven',
Sir Baptist Hicks funded the Market Hall in 1627.
It still dominates the heart of the High Street,
whose arches, pillars and high gables
neither time nor the weather disables.

The Market Hall we know well but what tales might it tell ?

In the seventeenth century, a feast of food,
grown and gathered around Campden -
butter, cheeses, milk, meat and poultry.
Oxen, donkey, horse hauling weighted wagons
of turnips, potatoes, cabbages, sprouts, onions.
What shouting, what trading, what bartering -
fresh eggs offered from smudged aprons;
holding high pink and white, plucked chickens;
and, surely, roses for ladies should they decide to call.

And could folk sleep on market days for sheep ?
The milling, the bleating, the barking, the shouting,
the calling, the laughing and the auctioneering !

Markets days the focal point of village life
and traders kept warm with banter and gossip,
while slowly twisting from the beams,
a fat goose. so tempting for dinner, chosen by merchants -
who believed they could always spot a winner.
Children playing and peeping around the pillars,
ever alert for stray apples as much needed 'fillers' !

No sweeter sound to the seasoned sellers
than coins rattling in their pots and pockets,
while wintry flakes swirl around the arches,
before the taking home of empty sacks and baskets,
and, perhaps, a wave and smile to the locals,
watching them wheeling their wares away

on a squeaking cart drawn by a much loved horse
bringing to the close another market day.
And, later, the scurrying of rats and prowling cats
seeking tit-bits in the silent, shadow-laden Hall.

Festive times were surely the best
whether Scuttlebrook Wake or the Olimpick Games,
what colours and costumes for carnivals and fetes,
from Scuttlebrook Queens to Morris Dancers.
And, what was relished by far the most,
the divine smell of a juicy, succulent pig roast;
or the hunter's horn calling his pack of yelping hounds
to where the red coated riders could be found.

Girls waving from pillars and along the arches
at local, voluntary soldiers on marches,
before they set sail for the horrors of the trenches.

And names from generations on the walls
tell another story of the Market Hall,
providing cover like a great makeshift shawl
for pouting pigeons, nesting swallows
and loitering lovers, laughing and whispering in the shadows,
as the moon's silvery beams settled along its hollows.

While Time, silently and relentlessly, slipped away
not only with the seasons but the centuries,
until we arrive here, today.

Where a family of Japanese tourists clearly adore
the thick ribs of the wooden beams, the puckered pillars,
and the well-worn, wonderfully uneven, stone floor.

And it seems, somehow, absolutely right
that those from far away should find such delight
in the Market Hall, forever serving,
again and again, the heart of Chipping Campden.

The Cabinet Maker

From the valleys and mountains of Wales,
A fine young man from Tonypandy set out
On a journey that led into England's heart.
He answered what was, surely, destiny's call,
To be carved and moulded in the craft and art
Of a Cabinet Maker. From training in Bristol
And, then, with his Welsh bride, the discovery
Of a new job and home at the Old Silk Mill,
In a Cotswold village called Chipping Campden.
In the late thirties often found working at home
With glue bubbling in a pot on wintry nights
And following revered craftsmen like a son,
Inheriting their skills and standards to carve
A decent future in the green and golden wold.
The skills of his craft, extended and absorbed.
He read a piece of wood as if it were a book.
Inferior quality analysed and judged by one look.
His measurements as precise with his eyes
As that with an instrument. His tools well-used.
They became a natural extension of his limbs.
His cabinets now acquired by connoisseurs.
Yet, among the most prized of all his carvings,
A work daily seen: the oak screens in St James'.
And the quality of his eye transferred to the lens,
Taking photographs sought by the Tourist Board:
And his range from Church to the Market Hall,
To legendary photos of locals like Jimmy Teapot.
Ever keen, this early pioneer of the camera club
And fire brigade member. Though, now, to keep
Busy as they say, the building of oak miniatures
For placement in a dolls house for their first
Great granddaughter - grandfather clock, chests,
Oak tables, four poster bed and a suite of chairs,
As prized as any made during his eighty years.
This master cabinet maker we'll not see again,
Whose gifts were perfected in Chipping Campden.

Heart of the Silversmith

The wheels of the old silk mill
Now stand silent and still.
But pass through the open door
And go to the second floor:

Find the silversmith intact,
Master of traditional skills:
Designer, modeller, chaser,
Engraver, turner, jeweller.

In the silversmith's workroom
Trusted traditions remain:
In the style and quality of work,
Classic standards maintained.

Hand and eye surgical-safe,
Silver sculptor, deft designer,
Launched from trusty bench
With chisels and hammers.

Selected from scores of stakes.
Iron heads bright as silver,
Which deliver a unique design
That shall endure for all time:

From loving cups and plaques
To crosses and chalices -
The silversmith displays his art,
So that it glistens in every heart.

Dry Stone Waller

Just after lunch, I pass the solitary dry stone waller.
Wrapped in two shirts, waistcoat, jacket, windsheeter.
His hands red from winds which rattle his creaking van.
A battered trilby hides grey hair. He always works alone.
His eyes blue as the frosty sky. His hands haul stones.
Core tools: mason's hammer, chisels, pick, crowbars.
Astutely selects from a shortlist of weathered stones.
His eyes and hands sculptors would understand.

Dry stone builder buffeted by winds all day. He strikes
A lonely ring from his seasoned hammer, smooth
As bone. The cold chisel on stone sings in the wind.
He blends with caw and calls of crows that strut and
And inspect the fallow, frosted field. Oolitic limestone
Blocks break open like nut shells. The working ration -
One to two, two to one, plugged by off-cut nuggets.
His concentration impervious to the biting east wind.

Behind him stretch thirty metres of restored stone wall.
A string guide ensures why its direction never veers.
A shallow cavity filled by large blocks secures the base.
Jumpers, interlocking stones, ensure the wall grows tall.
Each stone perfectly placed, crested by a line of toppers.
They sit up straight, fall and rise with the flow of the land.
So fitting, they interact like a golden chain, placed along
Green breasts and yellow fields ruled by a host of wings.

Such tales drawn from memories of old stone wallers:
Of one demanding kippers for his tea once a week.
The skins then placed across his hands to heal cuts.
Dry stone wallers built the beauty of the Cotswolds.
Families often found mending walls on Campden hills.
Father filling wall faces, children offering pinning chips,
Wife and mother securing the centres. The walls bound
Families together, strong as stone before any storm.

The Kiftsgate Stone

Following a January snowfall,
Rummage around hedges near Dover's Hill.
to discover the elusive, camouflaged, historic stone.

Then, yesterday, a bright April afternoon,
search again along the high road,
among trees and thicket -
not ten yards from the road,
within a singing wood, surrounded by fallen branches,
find the Symbol of the Law and State - the Kiftsgate Stone.

A stumpy, stubborn, shabby stone.
Tall as an infant child, older than nine centuries.
Strewn with ribbons, tufts of green moss,
dry lichen and a solitary runner of withering ivy.

Observe a deliberate hole, the length of my pen,
used to insert and hold a sword or staff.

The function of the stone:
to hold monthly open-court,
judge disputes, conflicts, feuds,
and keep council meetings
to debate local matters and customs

From the Kiftsgate Stone they heard
Major Proclamations from the king -
new taxes, new wars, new soldiers and new kings proclaimed -
The last being George 111 in 1760.

Though above Campden, the Kiftsgate Stone remains,
forgotten, alone. Its ancient significance hardly known.

Field Names

Status gained from the finest patch.
The names of owners' prize sites
Reflect physical attributes:

Bell Ground, The Bowsings,
Church Hitching, The Drifts,
Big Drift, Little Drift, Engles,
Farthing Green Piece, Lark Furlong,
Raspy Bottom, Saturday Furlong,
Slatters Patch, Upper Herril,
Whistle Ground.

Drifts are narrow, lie end to end,
And rarely yield to hoof or trotter.

Hitchings - sheep hurdle enclosures,
Or Bowsings to describe cattle stalls.

Each one fit for the title of a poem.

Robert's Route

For twenty one years, no less,
Until he retired at sixty six,
Robert Worvell left Guiting Power daily
To work at Farmington Quarry.

The master mason pedalled his bike
And for two decades was a familiar sight.
When Robert cycled through Cold Aston
Its said they set their clocks by him.

Six days a week he'd quietly cruise
And did he brake to share some news ?
Would Robert soon spot and know
The range of birds in a hedgerow ?

Did he smile at leaping lambs
And greet workers walking to farms ?
Did he see foxes or badgers play
Towards the end of the day ?

And when he grew older and slower,
Was he at one with the wold
Protected from ice and cold
By memories of fields green and gold ?

And, for us, the smaller things,
As his bicycle bell more loudly rings
Than his hammer and chisel,
Sounding a faint but triumphant knell.

Among the seeds, buds and shoots,
Robert's route fed his roots.
And did he sense a greater hand
As he pedalled his bike through the land ?

Rain on the Green

This April intends to break new rain records.
It pours and pours and pours and pours.
Stone slats coloured grey and brown
turn dripping black. Roofs release waterfalls.
Chimney pots, stout and sullen, endure their wash.
Clustered cottages sulk in the storm.
Rivulets emerge from the bank, flood the drains.
Even the war memorial cross is up against
a losing battle. The defunct iron water pump
glowers in the downpour. Its redundancy now
twice mocked. The spring to the Windrush
slurps over its banks. Bloated to excess.
Red and yellow tulips wilt beside spattered walls.
Cars on headlight beam, wiper blades criss-cross.
But battering rain does not douse local life -
The post office door remains open. Business
as usual, of course. The owner of a builder's van
can be heard from a half-open bedroom window.
Busily hammering as if plugging leaks.
A lady opens her cottage door, beats a mat
using the rain to rid hardly perceptible dust.
Then she brushes her puddled front steps.
An old couple brave the open green. Their coats
drenched but their tread quick. A man rushes out
to take a parcel from his car boot, runs back
indoors. Then the rain's black temper eases -
vents a light shower as if shaken by a wet dog.
Blackbirds emerge from a wisteria and clematis.
Three men meet and chat at the lane junction.
They glance at a passing car, return a wave.
Then they disperse, two heading for the pub.
A lady appears walking her black dog. His tail
wagging under the spitting sky. A blackbird
whistles as if calling the tulips to rise up again -
as the grey blanket floats away from the green.

Notice Board

April, 2012

Village Agents - Outreach Work for Deaf People

Snow Information - Snow Warden

North Cotswold Rural Watch

East Gloucestershire Mobile Library - Alternate Wednesdays

Frog Racing - Guiting Power Village Hall

Wanted for Rent. Workshop/Studio. Anything considered.
Artist seeks Studio in which to Paint.

Guiting Power. New Flag Appeal.
For the past two years the historic English Standard
has flown proudly and daily
from the Flag Staff on Top of the Tower
At St Michael's and All Angels Church, Guiting Power.
Inevitably the weather has taken its toll
and the original flag is beyond repair.

The Farmer's Arms - Now doing Take Away Fish n Chips

Open Gardens - The Queen's Jubilee Weekend,
Sunday June 3rd.

The Chestnut Sonnets

Spring

Spring begins with a wink and nudge,
As buds and leaves like green fires
Gather and glimmer, striving to aspire
For the chestnut to stir and budge.
From its slumber it starts again to grow,
When her brown arms turn green
And candles of white flowers are seen
To match the memory of lost snow;
And, within a few weeks, her splendour
Dominates all surrounding nature:
As she blooms and blossoms more,
And her buxom foliage turns mature
To swell and soar high into the sky
And nesting birds into her branches fly.

Summer

What other tree so much compares
With a chestnut when summer flows ?
Though Oak is King, his Queen shows
Favours she so generously shares:
Shade for sheep asleep under her wares,
Nuts from her flowers children stow.
Through summer she shimmers and glows,
Where small creatures create lairs.
Once robed she majestically surveys all.
Her beauty becomes a green beacon:
Spurs finer thoughts and awakens the call
To all the wonders trees have done -
Such blessings within our sight and touch
Like Nature's great chestnut church.

Autumn

Though its leaves wane and wither,
Autumn urges them to be at their best
For a harvest of hues to hover and glower,
Before they tumble to their rusted rest.
Autumn supplies their finest hour,
Enabling the chestnut to paint its crest:
Mingling red, yellow, pink, brown, orange;
Richer than an Old Master's palette.
A tantalising, visual feast of infinite range,
Merging dawn, noon and sunset;
And, still, its leaves constantly change,
No more beguiling can they possibly get;
Until, spent of colour, they finally fall,
To create a brittle rust carpet for us all.

Winter

Winter wields whiplash winds,
Strips the branches of every leaf.
Wicked wintry weather wins,
Causes majestic chestnuts grief.
Gales gather, gang-up and growl,
Bully bare branches seeking a fight.
Snow and frost unite together,
Linger on branches, fresh and bright.
Winter shakes a ferocious fist -
Mocks moulding gowns on chestnuts,
Unable to retaliate or resist
At the skinflint season of callous cuts.
Yet, in winter chestnuts recouperate,
Builds the buds that keeps them great.

The Cheltenham Gold Cup, 2010

It has to be seen to be believed -
As thousands engulf the course;
And every one hopes they've backed
The Gold Cup's winning horse !

When the shimmering runners emerge
They glisten and glow in the sun,
While bookies change the odds
On Gold Cup horses about to run !

By the press and media loudly foretold -
The Battle between Kauto Star and Denman,
Would be the 'War of the Wold' -
But Imperial Commander no one told !

The Gold Cup race would prove his greatest test.
Yet ranked third place at best.
Although, Imperial Commander
Would soon prove to be a true wonder !

Finally, the runners are ready to start -
The Jewel of the Final Festival Day,
And a roar from the crowd
Sends the runners on their way !

The two favourites receive a cheer
As they gallop past believing they'll get clear !
Though Imperial Commander plays it cool,
For soon he'll make the favourite feel a fool !

He never resorts to any tricks.
In fact he stays clear from the mix.
Keeping outside on the bank,
He stalks Denman, the towering 'tank' !

They thunder past the grandstand
To roars and screams and cheers,
And every jockey has one intent -
To surpass his pounding peers !

Suddenly, from the stand, comes a mighty yell,
When Kauto Star falls into Hell !
Denman increases his speed
For another win as the Gold Cup steed !

Across the stands and terraces
Cheers and screams combine,
As the pack thunders up the hill,
Ravenous for the finishing line !

But, then, Imperial Commander
Shows he's a classic contender -
He chases 'the tank' who he begins to pass,
Giving more gas than he's ever been asked !

Riding on, driving on, racing on -
Imperial Commander and Paddy Brennan !
And when they finally gallop clear,
Towards the winning post rise the cheers !

The Grandstand seems to shake
And all of Prestbury Park quakes,
As Imperial Commander kicks past the post,
And the rest of the field becomes toast !

All Naunton wants to give the Gold Cup a kiss,
Masterminded by Nigel Twiston Davis !
No greater claim, no greater bounty -
The Gold Cup is back in Cotswold country !

Shooting the Swastika

They packed their tents and bags
And carefully folded their swastika flags,
And from London they slipped away
To the Cotswold for a summer holiday !

They had rented land from a lady
Who never thought they were shady !
But the villagers felt they were no good
And, so, went to see them near the wood !

Men who fought in the First World War
Could hardly believe what they saw
For, there, hoisted over Guiting Power,
The Black Shirts had hoisted the swastika !

Village hearts churned at such a sight
For they knew that flag was just not right.
And so the Black Shirts they openly told
Only the Union Jack flew in the Cotswold !

But campers, in gleaming shirts of black,
Soon went on a hostile verbal attack,
And then the Black Shirts began to cheer
As their swastika fluttered high and clear !

Though the villagers did not turn away
Vowing to cut short the campers holiday !
They set about the tents with out delay
Which erupted into a memorable affray !

Then one man put a bullet clear,
Right through the swaggering swastika !
The Black Shirts complained at once
To a retired Sergeant of Stow Police.

"What flag are you talking about ?"
Asked the retired Sergeant.
"I can't see any flag ! Take another look,
For all he shot was a black old rook !"

The Black Shirts looked amazed
At their flag now limp and razed !
They didn't like losing and, so, no longer
Round the Cotswold would they be cruising !

The Guiting villagers knew
They'd fully repelled the grizzly crew
When, early that very next day,
The Black Shirts were seen quickly driving away.

The villagers felt righteously outraged
And, so, courage needed to be displayed,
Which, later, would be
Somewhat amplified on the international stage.

Heavenly Wings

For collectors' eyes
The Guiting Power Guide supplies
The list of Local Butterflies:

Speckled Wood, Wall Butterfly,
Ringlet, Marbled White,
Meadows Brown, Gatekeeper,
Small Heath, Painted Lady,
Small Tortoiseshell, Peacock,
Comma, Common Blue,
Holly Blue, Orange Tip,
Brimstone, Red Admiral,
Small Skipper, Cabbage White.

And others to respect,
though they have long left:
Rare and local Heath Fritillary,
Chalk Hill and *Adonis Blues,*
White Admiral and *Wood White.*

And also let's not forget
the nomenclatures of moths:
The Clouded Yellow,
Hummingbird Hawk.
And, with regret, far fewer
Black and *Red Burnet.*

And what delights
To see such
Rare and Heavenly sights !

West of Guiting

Wild flowers glow along the road-sides:
Yellow, red, white, blue and pink,
And in the wind able to wave and wink
At those confined to car rides.
Jewels placed besides rough hedges,
And for a few weeks they'll bloom,
Decorating the long road to Winchcombe.
Below stone walls and verges:
Spikey plantain, boastful dandelions,
Field speedwell, Cow's parsley,
Hare's foot clover, high red campions,
Foxgloves, willow herbs, tansy.
They ribbon the winding ways with beauty
And captivate as if its their duty.

Proposal

Hidden birds who sing freedom's song
Near tracks wild flowers thrive along;
And with you, among such things,
That may lead to an exchange of rings.

Moreton Marketeers

Purchases reveal extent of spending power:
A quarter pound of cheese, two apples,
Or using a stall to shelter under the shower.
Bored children, half swing around stall poles.
Their eyes returning to the packets
Of sweets, boxed in bundles, two for a pound.
And, then, asked if some cut price carpets
Are the right colours to suit their bedrooms.
The colours *they* like are mustard and tomato -
Like they squirt on lunchtime hot-dogs !

Older couples shuffle between the linen
And the china. Spot yet another plate, its place
Already envisaged for cakes in the garden.
Watch the furrowed brows of young mothers
At the stall with baby clothes. Pram-jams
Occur, but its such enjoyable, bustling company.
Its just the cost triggering back-pocket alarms.
Sit in the cafe for a smoke and tea for those
Whose basic strategy is to keep down debt
As they light up another cut-price cigarette.

Pensioners totter along from the coach
To hunt in packs; keen to attack all stalls, set
To apply what seems a clear approach -
Only buy what they like and if they can afford it !
China tapped, held up for inspection by the sun.
Fruit checked out by six decades of inspecting.
Some prefer a bag of chips, others a cream bun.
They all return well-pleased to a warm coach.
Best of all the purchase of favourite sweets
As a gift but, then, eaten once they're seated.

The well-dressed couples wear leather shoes,
Levis, discreet jewellery, move slowly around
The stalls as though sifting out bargain clues.

Comparing costs from shops in local towns.
Their fingers run over raffia bags, weaved mats.
Finally plump, at last, for fresh peaches
While their husbands listen to sellers' yells,
Before following well-pleased spouses
To a coffee in highly recommended hotels.
They soon lose interest watching passers-by,
Glare at the grey sky and suggest holidays.

Single shoppers stand out easily
In the milling crowd - often turning, halting.
Some seem in a self-determined hurry,
Quick to buy and leave. Precision shopping -
A mackerel, teacloth. Always single items.
Avoid the bulging bags, keep one step ahead
Of what is expected - stimulated by whims,
Nurtured by being in, belonging to a crowd.
Then they get stuck between a family crush.
Appear even sadder as they smile and blush.

And the day-tripping families who look
Bemused by all the stalls that seem
To be straight out of a baby's picture book:
Flapping colours, bargains by the ream
That soon weave a spell over them -
Whether to buy combs, cups, mats, plants, a jar
Or home-made pots of marmalade or jam.
Buy enough to fill the boot of their car.
And, then, so tired, they sit on a wall, sifting chips.
Before returning to buy bargain priced xmas gifts.

Camera happy tourists spill onto the street,
Giggling at close shaves with tooting cars;
For some this is their holiday highlight treat -
Buying coats, leather bags, crease proof trousers.

They compare prices during lunch in a pub,
Laden with things that only a holiday can bring,
Displayed between half pints and hot grub.
Holiday shopping better than any other thing.
And finally the final laugh at the group photo call,
With a farewell kiss blown to the owner of a stall.

Dawn-starting stall holders devour bacon rolls.
The butcher with a white apron over his shorts
Jokes with a waitress outside the Resedale Hall,
Towering over the glittering canopies that skirt
The perimeter of the Fosse Way - leading out
Of the town, crammed with drivers itching to race
Ahead, to be among the first to scout the market.
They grab the best bargain - a free parking place.
The queues of coaches, buses, lorries and cars
Make Moreton Market the Sun for attracting stars.

Tuesday Entertainment

It was never ever meant to be this way,
But often amuses non-drivers they say,
Watching car drivers search
For a rare car-parking perch
On Moreton in Marsh Market Tuesday !

Curfew Tower

Crooked and bent and curved,
Stands where the traffic swerves.
It almost appears out of place,
Beside wheel pounding commerce
And glistening, business signs
That signify modern times.

But late on a windy, wintry night
The little tower seems so right.
Especially below the half moon,
Or catching the early rising sun.
It becomes a breathing building,
At home with its head dozing.

Market Day offers it a stage
To contrast with strident stalls.
Stirs a reminder of another age.
Children claim the tower curls,
And leans to eavesdrop
Over traffic that hardly stops.

It withstands all attempts to go.
Star attraction of the Town Show.
Yet, somehow, keeps its hold
From times it turned hearts cold,
When its bell broke the town calm,
Sounding the dreaded fire alarm.

Divine Justice

Of course, there were the poor areas
and families in desperate situations.
Now classified as 'socially disadvantaged'.
But, in such situations, the ways of the Lord
could intervene in the most dramatic way.

Take, for example, the local rector,
who tried to prevent a drunken husband
from assaulting his wife, by advising the husband
to assume the behaviour and morals
of a Christian life. Perhaps, an early example of
'counselling the instigator of domestic violence'.

But all wise advice and careful counselling
by the Rector did not halt the husband's violence.

And, so, it came to pass, when, yet again,
the poor wife was badly beaten up
by her drunken husband,
the Rector went to the house and felt compelled
to apply the Old Testament proverb,
'an eye for eye, a tooth for a tooth',
or, in this case,'a black eye for a black eye,
a broken tooth for a broken tooth',
by, firstly, removing his clerical collar,
and then 'soundly thrashing' the husband.

Such action would now, of course, be considered
'morally reprehensible.
Indeed, an outrageous abuse of a trusted position.'

However, following the Rector's 'response',
no further violence was recorded
as being inflicted by the husband on his wife.

'John Bunyan the Second'

Mr. John Mann, was born in Baddington, Suffolk.
He trained for the Ministry at Hoxton Academy
and on graduation was appointed, in 1801,
as the First Minister of Moreton in Marsh
Congregational Church. He delivered his first sermon
in a barn before it was converted to a meeting house.
Fifty years later, he retired from his Ministerial post
due to ill-health. But in that half century, he united
and boosted— the growing congregation in the town.
Reverend Mann's zeal and energy became legendary.
His belief helped him overcome all obstacles -
from arson in the Hall to abuse from disbelievers.
He never faltered and like the Good Shepherd
he protected his flock. He gave inspiring guidance.
His mission in Moreton spread the free gospel
which led to the conversion of future generations.
He set up the first school for children of Dissenters.
His sermons were written in tiny handwriting
but when delivered they cast a giant shadow.
Travelling on horseback he spread the Gospel
across the Cotswold from Shipston to Broadway.
His sermons lightened the poverty and darkness
of those who worked long, back-breaking hours
in farms and fields and villages; and who came to value
his uplifting words. He raised their aspirations
and spread the Good News across the countryside.
He became known as 'John Bunyan the Second'.
His steadfast faith won communities. He gave support
and strength to so many families, and such a title
would have been well-judged and fully deserved.
And what better employer could he have served ?

Source: 'The History of Two Centuries of Christian Fellowship
at the Congregational Church, Moreton in Marsh'
(1796 - 1996) by W. Edward Francis and Gwen Booth

Frozen Images '47

'We were put in these nissan huts,
near Moreton in Marsh,
as we had no-where else to go.
Winter, forty seven was so cold.
Like Siberia, honest.
At bedtime I used to dress the kids up
as if they were going out. Extra woolens,
trousers, the lot. Even put on their gloves.
Then I used to lay with them,
trying to give them a bit of my warmth.

I remember breathing on the baby's head
and seeing my breath freezing on her hair.

When I took a glass of water to bed
by the time I put it on the table it had frozen.

I remember licking the ice when I was thirsty.'

Memories of The Great Freeze, January, 1947,
in Nissan Huts, Moreton in Marsh.

Darts Team Photograph

The four men represent the Darts Team.
From an age when it was the fashion
To wear a suit, shirt, collar and tie.
Representatives of the winning season.
They smile as if they had won the FA Cup.
And to a local pub it meant as much as that.

They sit together, holding a glistening trophy.
Proud of their achievement. Each man
Would have served in the Forces. Hair styles
Kept to short back and sides. Except the youngest.
Slashed back hair, glistens with cream.
Rock and Roll already redefining horizons.

Stalwarts of the days when each village
Had a pub that could launch a darts team.
In competition every throw earned its silence.
Star players were prized in villages.
Those were the days when they'd play games
Using darts made from six inch nails.

Perhaps, such hands once held arrows,
Drew back the twine on longbows,
Belonging to the most feared archers in Europe.
Despite being outnumbered,
They were crucial in winning battles for kingdoms.
And still keep their deadly hand-eye coordination.

After Ploughing

Plough make-over complete -
    Brown ribs, straight and neat.
Worth stopping to take a look,
    Raked by rummaging rooks.

Soon it shall all turn green,
    Rise as waving autumn corn.
Now its glowing after dawn.
    A field just up from little Dorn.

Those bristling blades did so well,
    Though too few around to tell.
And the way the earth now turns,
    Like slices off a beef roast fallen.

Across the lane a mouse runs,
    Hides in the hedge from the sun.
Takes a high risk out of burrows,
    Teeming below flashing furrows.

Feel the rising sun hardening,
    As if squeezing sap glistening
On the curled, sun-burnt slabs.
    Everything wants its ‘fair grabs’ -

Even strangers relish the field,
    Rampaging rooks won’t yield.
Yet will be taken off the brown stage
    To be strewn on a poem’s page.

Pedigree Herefords

Their marquee holds over fifty stalls
On a grassy floor draped in yellow straw.
Iron rails and bales serving as walls
To contain champions laden with awards.
Cattle smells and sounds all absorbing
To visitors entering, gently stepping -
Entranced by the brown and white array,
Enhancing whatever field they roam.
Cow and calf each convey
The divine union between bulk and beauty.
'Well, something close to near a ton,'
A farmer declares estimated weight.
When over fifty tons congregate.
On laying down they seem to expand
Like a brown and white boulder over the land.
Yet the impact of being close to such mass
Causes children to gently touch, caress.
As though sensing in their stability,
Titanic strength and substantial security.
Nothing else can be easily compared
Or display an equal, all-encompassing stare.
How their black-brown eyes disarm,
Contain an innocent, child-like charm;
And such effeminate, long, white eyelashes
Arouse from spectators 'instant crushes'.
What's more the snow white flesh
Of a calf would make an angel seem flushed.
They cast a steady, baleful gaze,
That holds a different, deeper kind of maturity
Which awakens our commercialised humanity,
As we listen to their occasional lowing
And watch their patient, measured movements,
Drawing comfort from their predictable ways
That slows us down to savour more our days.

The Supreme Dictator

If you enter the Moreton Show at Gate One,
just before the first tent devoted to shopping,
expect to meet a four legged family second to none:
under an oak pen lies Mr and Mrs Saddleback,
their six piglets hovering within a bee's breath of their mum.

Their Dad's full name matches
any blue-blooded aristocrat -
Bunkershill Glascote Dictator the Seventeenth.

Dictator's main meal is cereal
but he likes a daily treat of fruit - plums particularly.
His finger-long tusks love grappling with apples.
He's over half a hundred weight and the tallest pig around.

He only loses his temper if another male
comes into his territory. Then its out with the tractor,
which never fails to push him out of the way.
Although he'll still try to push it over !

Dictator's harem has no borders.
He's chased the Grand Duchess with a branch in his mouth,
cornered her against the fence,
and, there, promptly sired more heirs and heiresses.

He also likes rolling around on the ground.
His tusks pluck up best Moreton turf,
over which he slithers and slides and wriggles,
before he decides to settle down again.

He loves being stroked just above his ears.
A sensitive spot which relishes a warm hand.
So much so, that if stroked in the field
(as some handlers have found),
Dictator simply slumps to the ground !

Singing on Sunday

Hymns honoured Sunday mornings,
Along with starched collars, best hats, polished shoes.
Glistening children in their Sunday best.
Their voices seemed like angels to familial ears.

The weather determined the afternoon,
when singing was heard again,
perhaps, blackbirds enjoyed the competition,
when the family took their walks down favoured lanes;
or attending Catechism, or the Mann Institute
for PSA - Pleasant Sunday Afternoon.

In the evening, the family gathered in the parlour
where their mother, a trained soprano and pianist,
rendered arias, lieder and traditional English folk songs.

Her daughters sung accompanying verses,
while the choruses were sung by all the family.
The men provided a contrasting but pleasing bass chorus.

The elder daughter was in the local school choir,
and won First Prize among county schools
at the final stage held in Gloucester Cathedral.

In later years, she played piano duets with her mother.
And Grandpa, of course, who would listen and watch,
occasionally joined in a verse or two,
though his trumpet lay dormant;
once highly prized in the Moreton Brass Band.

After an aria or song or hymn or trumpet solo,
the children would be in bed by seven.
But, then, Family Singing started to fade
and finally fell silent soon after the war.

Flood, July 2007

It thundered down the hill.
Swept across the Fosse Way.
Poured into shops, offices, pubs, houses.
Caused chaos in the town.
You couldn't stop it.
Nothing could stop it.
Some people pushed cushions against front doors.
But what's a cushion against tons of raging water ?

It tumbled down corridors,
swamped cellars, ruined businesses.
The smell was just as bad.
A lifetime of being house proud
scuttled in a few hours.
Old people had to be rescued.
Cut off the town, cut off the railway line.
It was like the town had been devil cursed.

And after the shock. The start of something else -
which proved stronger than the flood.
In fact, a different flood.
with as much power as the flood of water.
A Welcome Flood of Kindness -
Neighbours looking after neighbours.
with offers of help, sympathy, support
and the sharing of food, blankets, beds.

In the massive clearing up
locals looked out for each other.
A deeper, battling spirit overcame
those stressed and those in distress.
The Flood of Fortitude proved stronger,
being Alive and Well
and found all over Moreton in Marsh.
The flood strengthened the community's heart.

'The City of Dorn'

i

A hamlet of nine houses, full of farming stock,
that shielded a greater mystery - 'the City of Dorn';
waiting, resting, buried just beneath those gilded,
green, golden, long, long ago childhood summers.
Partially unfurled when the farmer of two daughters
granted permission to the Colonel and his wife, an
archaeologist recently returned from Ravenna, Italy,
to excavate a corner of pastured fields, and to finally
quench or celebrate the rumours of 'Roman remains'.

ii

The dig would delicately excavate tantalising things
left by a vague settlement serving dusty chariots;
weary legions, parched in the high wolds, earning
replenishing hours beside a scorching Fosseway:
Sipping wine from cups of clay, feasting, swapping
war stories, then tossing aside their empty plates
as prized as Incas gold in future days. The symbols
of their presence, their state, their dispensation ,
when the known world knelt before Roman ways.

iii

Within a week bound by distribution of marking tape
around what appeared, photographed from the air,
paler outlines deemed the legion city's possible walls.
Two huts erected, one for digging tools, equipment,
the other for habitation. And the Colonel's chauffeur,
on call every weekend of those three golden summers,
pictured leaning on a spade, in rolled-up shirtsleeves,
but retaining his tie and peaked cap, as if to declare
he was just as loyal as any centurion to his Colonel.

iv

But, slowly, the edges of the old city gently uncovered -
'pale blue corridor walls; ash from an earlier building;
the finding of first to fourth century coins, a butt beaker,
red samian pottery from Gaul'. Unauthorised helpers,
local children, explored the sides of treasured trenches,
gleefully taking their 'finds' to the Colonel and his wife.
But then politely halted, unless adults were present,
so that no further 'innocent invaders' stormed 'the city'.

v

And the other, completely unexpected excavation,
the quality of kindness shown by the Colonel's wife -
who helped to bathe their daughter in vinegar, when
badly stung by nettles; and the other, older daughter,
thrown by her pony, her skull fractured, and was
tended by the Colonel's nurses; who had cared for
their fourteen year old son, sadly lost to leukaemia.
The day nurse stayed on to support the daughter,
whose recovery was thought 'immeasurably aided'
by hampers packed and dispatched from Harrods !

vi

And still the City of Dorn released further secrets:
two wells in particular, that held what some roman
or cotswolder had slipped, or deliberately dropped,
into what was held surely the safest of all depths -
a lady's beads and silver from a lover or husband.
Other discoveries included - bone needles, ironwork.
And sent to the British Museum: 'two steel yards; a
meat-spit; a threshing floor paved in small pebbles';
also, discovered by the elder, delighted daughter,
the prize of 'a brick-oven with bricks still inside it'.

vii

Perhaps, dissembled in the dig - deeper judgements:
the fleetingness of fortune, the value of present time,
helped to nurture the friendship between the Colonel,
his wife and the two daughters. Later, Christmas gifts
exchanged besides photographs of their distant digs.
A friendship that held, and proven later, when the
girls were invited to the Colonel's estate, escorted to
the roman collection in the conservatory, before taken
upstairs to where the Colonel's wife lay bed-stricken;
but, somehow, rallied sufficiently to greet the girls,
though her condition allowed only a short, final visit.

viii

Without his wife, the Colonel did not return to Dorn.
After the war the dig was filled in, the land returned
to its brown and gold and green. Though the spades
and trowels did not rust, often used by the daughters'
in their own gardens, while holding memories of those
excavations among 'the treasured trenches', briefly
unveiled in that long ago summer in 'the City of Dorn'.
And, equally memorable, the finding and the building
Among the ashes and embers of the Roman Empire,
A childhood friendship like a legionnaire's beacon light,
That throughout their daughters' lives burned bright.

Unrecorded Traffic Fatality

Driving out of Moreton a dead pheasant
lies on the road.
Just been hit.
Its gold, brown, black, green feathers
look like a squashed bouquet.

Hugging the kerb
another pheasant hovers,
unsure what to do.
Bereft of her stricken mate.
She struts about in a stressed state.

Her head askew,
wondering what to do.
She's in terminal shock.
Distress, shock, grief
Causes her to stagger like a drunk.

Then a magpie and crow appear.
Ravenous roadside undertakers.
She can't stop them
As they hop toward her dead partner.
Their beaks sharp as scalpels.

Great Tit Call Out

Near St David's church he makes his call,
Silvery tones meant to wake one and all.
He rings the peal for Nature's sacred bell
And one we have come to know so well.
He leaves his precious, entwined bed
For lime branches he far prefers instead,
To herald the advent of the Great Glow,
Openly summons the winter sun to show.
His call of 'teacher, teacher' those discern
Who, from him, desire to arise and learn,
As fresh light reveals his yellow breast
And a black stripe he wears like a crest.
The Great Tit, once again, calls us forth
As song and sunlight bring the day's birth.

St David's Spire

Soars out from limes and sycamores,
A fawn cone among green.
Dominates Evenlode's low shores.
High Prince of the sky scene.

And, then, when it seems so near,
It conspires to disappear -
Shielded by roofs and trees along a lane.
Before it rises, triumphant, again.

Dowdleswell Beeches

Obviously, its the sort of thing
You certainly expect to see in the Spring:
A row of beeches, tall and slim,
Each branch the smoothest of any tree limb.

But these beeches in another sense
Rise high and aloof, behind a long stone wall,
Which also serve as their defence
From where so many birds sing and call.

Their leaves emerald-green and bright,
Glisten in the morning light;
And such is their blanket of green
It may be among the finest ever to be seen.

And in the autumn, it must be said,
Once again, I chose this road instead,
And found their red hues proved such a sight,
They made me stop in wonder and delight.

And, so, I share them with you,
For they are a stunning sight to view:
The splendour of autumn hues teaches
Life is wonderful beside Dowdleswell Beeches.

Daffodils of Sapperton

The symbol of Spring excels
In the lambing month of March.
Spring winds shake yellow bells
Below oak, ash, maple, beech.

Their green and yellow colours
Always delight when they arise,
Freed from winter's dour hours
By daffodils Spring recognised.

Spring's delights rise anew -
In this village daffodil-jewelled:
Glistening beneath the sky-blue
Where Spring's beauty is held.

On ledges, gutters and sills,
Blackbirds hover and sing,
Near the swathe of daffodils
And the goats by 'The Bell Inn'.

Daffodils display their trumps -
A welcome platoon on the verge.
Their yellow and green clumps
Mingle and marry and merge.

Breezes shake each yellow bell,
Which should ring every heart,
Sensing what daffodils foretell:
Herald when Spring shall start.

An Uncommon Commoner

Whether on humble path or remote way
Its found on a summer's day.
Yet, since ancient times, declared a herb,
Its praises down the ages heard !
A measured extract taken from this plant
(Whose delight is constant),
Might favour release from depression
And those of mute expression.

So, allow us to claim
For this yellow saviour another name:
'An uncommon saviour let it be known
when selected and grounded down.'
A good and caring sort -
No Commoner is 'Common St. John's Wort' !
For she wields such power,
Uncommon on a common wild flower.

Troublesome Tongues !

The Village School was such a success
But one thing was omitted from its prospectus
Regarding the adjacent field, whose dairy herd
Often interrupted the teacher's word !
Caused the children to turn as one -
Delighted by the distraction !
When the adjacent field of jersey cows
Licked dew off their classroom windows !

The Peacock of Quenington

Straight and long runs the Quenington Lane
Which I use, now and again.
This morning as I'm driving back home,
I see on the grass verge, strutting alone,
A peacock on parade and grown full-size !
Although he's such a splendid surprise,
I wonder why he's landed here
And throw him bread crumbs because he's so near.

His long, royal blue neck earns a sight
For its brighter and richer than the summer sky.
Even so, his glistening coal black eye
Detects my hidden sandwich supply.
However he's unsure, whether its a wheeze,
And keeps his distance between the hedge and trees.
No bird seems more majestic or more finer.
No wonder they delighted the mandarins of Ancient China.

I pause without a clue
Confronted by a neck of royal blue,
And a fabulous fan of circles of blue, gold and fawn
That would grace a Cotswold mansion lawn.
In fact, when I reflect and take stock
He displays colours that act like an electric shock,
Especially when found down a lonely country lane
Which I drive down now and again.

I hope he'll avoid any harm
So I drive down to the nearest farm.
Out from the barn the farmer appears
And soon allays all my fears.
He says 'the peacock's been around for years'
And never caused anyone any tears.
He's one of two whose survived everything -
Traffic, shotguns, pesticides and whatever winter brings.

Lamping

I heard this account from a fourteen year old
lad from Lechlade.

About ten at night
he joined his sister's boy-friend
in the back of a jeep, which was driven
across the fields.

They shone their torches into the night,
and picked out the shining eyes
of deer and badgers.

Their purpose was to find the fox
before he killed any more sheep.

The boy followed two of the men
towards a clump of bushes,
growing near the old boundary wall.

They thought the fox might be in the bushes
until one of them men,
quite casually,
shone his flashlight over the wall.

The light immediately fell on the fox.
Silently sitting there,
hardly daring to move.

He still didn't move when they levelled
their shotguns at him.

Two Buzzards

Near Shipton they hover
Above, as if spun from the sun,
two black specks, slowly swirling.
Riding warm currents in the March sky.
Scanning the earth for victims.

Among riddled fields
with shoots of wheat,
small things cower -
field mice, voles, lizards,
forewarned by the songbirds' silence.

Until the velocity of their descent -
comparable to a supersonic impact.
The sudden spike in the neck
and wrench from a beak.
Death by avian jet express.

How to Deceive a Partridge

A two-poacher task -
one flew a cunning kite
which made the partridges freeze
believing it a bird of prey.

The covey of partridges would hug the ground
as the 'carnivorous kite'
soared and hovered in the wind,
'ravenously surveying' the cowering prey.

Scared off other birds, too -
pigeons, pheasants, plovers, pee-wits
on seeing the partridges scuttle and scurry for cover.

Poacher Two then walked toward
the covey of petrified partridges
who, on hearing him approach,
were forced to break cover -

as they fluttered into the sky,
still fearing the sky-high hunter -
they were brought down by the poacher's gun !

In those not too faraway days,
a kite helped put food on desperate tables.

Keeping a Copse

Another way farmers raise much needed cash
is to sell what's often seen but hardly noticed -

a copse, small meadow,
scarcely profitable in the centre of a field.

Just stands out like a green oasis in a brown desert.
A few thousand pounds would purchase the wood.

The contract states the copse must be kept 'intact'.
No development allowed of any kind.

The new owner will need to walk across
great rolling fields to gain access to the wood.

An open-plan home without rooms, without comforts.
But the hardest thing, of course,

to confront himself,
without identity tags - job, car, status, family.

Strange at first - engulfed by trees.
Although, an opportunity to reflect and plan.

Slowly, he will learn
how to look and listen and to smell the copse.

Observe the fleeting residents: birds, squirrels,
rabbits, stoats. Maybe badgers, even deer.

Its like building a new relationship.
But, this time, no-one and nothing will let him down.

Within a few months the relationship becomes so fulfilling,
he'll want to 'move in' with his 'magical mistress'.

Ticklin' Trout

'All you do,' said the old fisherman,
'is pick some shade, so u'r shadow can't be seen.

You'll see ole Mista Trout afore 'e sees you,
coz you're on top lookin' down -

Jus' like the Lord !
And you also got sum Power o'er Life, too !

So when 'e comes along, u slips u'r 'ands
in the river like slidin' under a baby's 'ead.

Now wait for trout to lay over u'r 'and.
'e'll do that as sure as the sun !

Then, u tickles its belly. Like stroking a leaf.
'onestly, 'e'll lap it up ! Trouts love a tickle !

Then u opens u'r 'and
and scoops 'im clean out of the water !

As 'e wriggles on the bank,
I like to think old trout is laughin' 'imself silly !

So much so, 'e 'ardly notices the cosh
comin' down to crush 'is 'ead !"

Adder

I was already looking down
on the rough straw track,
and listening to the sound of my dusty boots
tramping over scattered straw.

And, then, not a metre from me,
I spotted what seemed a darker, patterned,
oddly twisted branch,
and yet more more angled than any branch
deposited on the yellow verge of the field.

I almost passed,
then stopped to look,
and in those two seconds -
sufficient to sense some threat,
the branch curled up one of its ends,
then its whole body shook like a brown whip
and, before I could half-turn,
it slithered like a brown blade into the cut corn
and was gone !

Only its colour and length and rustle in the cut grass
revealed it was an adder I had passed.
And then I looked across the shorn field,
wondering what death I had caused
for I driving him in there,
and now everything in that close-cropped field
needed to be on full alert.

For there was no favours or friendship
in the way it

froze then flashed then fired.

And also triggered some fear in me.
What if it had directed its writhing speed and fangs
more seriously ?
I could never match its instinctive escape.

Though it seeks and sinks its venom into smaller things -
vole, lizard, field mouse, small bird.

But do you envy any of them
who daily risk such an ambush ?
Those beautiful brown and patterned rings
are the dress of death to halt breath and song.
Yet who should judge behaviour in the wild
where there resides no right nor wrong ?
Out here, what shows life
affirms beauty and freedom
on the rim of nature's merciless knife.

Yellow Wagtail

She stops alert on the bush,
   Furnace yellow like the dusk.
Issues her chirruping snatch
   You have to be quick to catch.
Then, like a sun flash, is gone
   To snuggle deep among corn.
But a fleeting spurt of yellow
   No brighter flag could billow;
Shades all else August shows.

Evenlode Horses

First time in weeks the evening is dry,
a spin around Evelode brings a halt
near a field below the pale evening sky,
where six horses stand and wait
unconcerned until I arrived. Grazing
and standing together, solitary, still.

And they watch me watching them together
separated by a great green field,
where dock leaves sprout with buttercups,
emblems of the untilled field.
Seven horses waiting for feed,
though attention is something also needed.

They are a comforting, goodly sight
seeming richer when the sun goes down.
Their colours of grey and black,
chestnut, fawn, honey brown
contrast with the bushes and hedges,
but each player a master among green stages.

A blackbird flies out from the hawthorns,
whistles over the grass. Other songs, too,
filter around. Two courting pigeons
sweep over the field, high then low,
settle behind cover provided by a beech tree,
where they continue to coo beyond sight or reach.

The foal has not moved one hoof
but the mares turn aside from the gate,
while the grey continues to eat, quite aloof,
from her green, buttercup decorated plate.
Finally, I turn to go, though not one word did we say,
yet serves as the perfect encounter to close the day.

The Woods of Bledington Heath

When the roe-buck darted out of the woods
Onto the track I knew I had to follow him back.
I slipped through the gap but once in the woods
Found the light suddenly dim and drab and dark,
The kind of place a roe-buck would like to roam
And, I suppose, just right if you want to be alone.

But the path was littered with broken branches
And brown, yellow leaves half-starved in August.
Tall and thin, twisted and grim, forgotten trees
Seemed either to huddle or fight for the sunlight
That falls in white slanted angles, here and there,
Through the canopy as if by some miser spared.

And then a gathering of pines whose needles
Had stock-piled so it felt like a rich man's carpet,
Where I stood to see what might suddenly rustle.
But the sound of softly breaking branches stopped.
What I was listening for was also listening silently
And, I felt, was far safer, wiser watching out for me.

Hoof-prints on the track had formed rain-pockets.
Small things might seek to warily drink from them.
Then the leaves right above me started to rustle,
And a squirrel looked down as if waiting for some
Response, then scarpered higher into the green,
Triggering a magpie to break out from its screen.

Soon the track became a fork of alternative ways
And to me implied, here, I could no longer remain,
Too much distracting the residents on full display:
And a dismayed jay decided to constantly complain
Of the stalking interloper, mis-cast underneath,
Barracking the wild theatre woods on their heath.

Kingham Characters

And where can they be found now
Characters so many used to know ?
Only by those who care to look
Through the pages of an old book !
There they live waiting for our Age,
Leading players of their village -
Who knew their place on the scales
And fit for 'The Canterbury Tales':

i

Kingham claimed as its divine ruler
No kinder or wiser than the Rector,
Who aspired to the role of squire
From local lands astutely acquired.
And then farmed God's little glebe
For in such possessions he believed.
He was a good man of the cloth and
Quietly applied his divine authority.
And ministered equally to one and all
Especially those his wife invited to call.

ii

The Rector's wife was christened
The 'Queen of Kingham' instead
By certain young men of the gentry,
Who sauntered in Kingham society.
They relished her dinner offers
And were ideal as discreet tasters,
Especially of her liqueur wines which
Could be apple or grape or peach.
But their favourite was damson gin.

She distributed loaves and wine
To villagers who declared her kind.
From her behaviour it was easy to tell
Queen Victoria was her role model !
She upheld all that was good and true
In whatever she attempted to do!

iii

The Schoolmaster was always keen
And stressed the utmost discipline,
Where children were drilled in things
That only the three Rs surely brings.
His pupils soon knew all they should
Which also made Inspectors feel good.
But, if not, despair was felt everywhere
Though that, of course, was truly rare.
His learning was shrewd, deep, wise
And dunces disliked as much as lies;
While good manners held equal to
Almost anything else his pupils knew.

iv

And Captain Barrow, the Boer's son,
Also deserves a favoured mention -
Whether up the snowy Alps ascending,
Or Kingham pupils marching, drilling.
He also taught village folk on a slope
How to climb with an ice-axe and rope.
After that, how to expertly cut ice steps.
And ended displays with cash lumps
Which attracted far too many tramps !
He detested all doctors, lived till ninety
And supped stout and port twice daily.

He converted the rectory into a ship -
Each dawn the red ensign hoisted.
Though 'The Times' printed extracts
From his diary recording Kingham days,
Remains entirely intact and accurate,
And the Bodleian Library displays.

v

Keeper Cook wore a night-cap
Whose tassel was gently taken up,
For his old hands were far too thin
To be shaken by friends visiting him.
Yet, when young, found in field fallow
The nest and lay of the stone curlew.
He believed Blucher won Waterloo
And Wellington only waltzed through !

vi

What a postman was Tom Phipps,
Daily walked twenty three miles
In snowstorms never seen to slip !
Always in song and with a smile.
He sang superbly and when reciting
He made music with all the words.
He noticed all the birds and flowers
As though they were his neighbours.
And once when deep in Bruern Wood
Saw a pine martin hunting for food.
As a young lad he rose really early
To play cricket before work begun.
He raised a large family and came
From one of ten of the same name.

So much so, his father took his tenth
Babe to the Squire believing, as they
Applied in those days a legal tithe -
Whether tenth egg or tenth sheath -
His Lordship would also relieve him
Of the tithe for his tenth and final son !

vii

And the retired, married inn-keeper
Who turned a deep and true believer.
He went to church Sunday morning,
Then the afternoon and the evening,
As if to miss any service was a crime !
As though making up for the time
He had called but now He was calling,
And never needed a second telling !
Though raised a pet lamb so nice,
But after the butcher's axe never ate
When offered one tiny tender slice -
For ale never fouled his fine heart.

viii

Three carriers, brothers all lame,
Knew too little but played a game
With their donkey when it rained.
(If laden with rail passengers bags
And names clearly inserted on tags)
Might deposit such bags in a ditch
For passengers to furiously search !

ix

Porter was the village all-rounder:
Carpenter, carrier, snow clearer,
Gardener, hedger, waller, plumber.
But too often forgot to ask payment
And so fell far behind with his rent,
Causing frequent changes of address
But all his homes remained a mess !
He carried home wasps' nests,
But fought them when they burst
And zoomed around the room !
Porter carved the villagers' coffins
And led the funeral processions.
He even won a royal bravery award
For saving a local 'poor mad girl'
Fallen down a poisonous well.
He loved his old fowls and pony
Which, at forty, still survived him -
For he could never kill any of them.
While his widowed wife often cried
To feed her cats that over multiplied.

Foxholes Hedgerow

'Foxholes Only' painted on a rough old sign
Summon me to turn and walk down the track,
Hoping to see what's termed a parallel course
Of the shy, withdrawn, reclusive Evenlode
Before escaping over the plains of Oxfordshire.
But a lordly hedge guards and defends any view.
And what a royalist hedge ! Some ten foot high
That soars along the entire stretch of the track.

On the river side its unbroken, except for
Two gateways revealing waving corn fields.
But the hedge dominates, laid back and cut
As close as that of any lawn. Its sloping angle
Long combed and cultivated by whistling winds,
Could easily be summer's green, frozen wave
About to cap and curl before it crashes down.

Though this hedgerow will never tumble down
Having mortar far stronger than any stone wall
Comprising hawthorns, blackthorns, alders,
Sycamores, brambles, briars, thistle and rowan.
They knit and bind and tuck, weaving branches
Stronger than chains. They will not rot or rust
For the seasons replenish it. And this hedge
Is of such splendour reared by trusted owners,
Who have yearly tended and kept and protected
Its growth and grooming down the centuries.

But much more than a hedge, an emerald ribbon;
A treasured possession as valued as their crops;
A guardian and proven stalwart of the estate.
It fittingly dominates this lonely, old, single track.
Fire its only true enemy, otherwise it possesses
The strength and character to combat and survive
Winter storms, spring floods, summer drought.

Yet, plays the bounteous parent supplying
Homes for endless, vibrant, frequent wild life -
Already signalled by a burst of dipping martins,
Whose winged acrobats seem an aerial salute
To illustrious green walls of the castled fields,
Shrouding and shielding the running Evenlode.
The hedgerow is the guardian of a river princess.

This is the hedgerow as strong as a castle wall.
This is the hedgerow that'll never wither or fall
For its been kept by those who lived all their days
Cultivating and keeping the best of country ways.

Our Lady's Little Glass

As though anyone would ever need
The support of bindweed,
Unwanted among fields and hedgerows
Where it humbly aspires to grow.
But, now, discover how it came to pass
To be christened, 'Our Lady's little glass':

A waggoner who carried wine casks
Hauled by six oxen, so fit for the task,
Was forced to halt due to a muddy track
And so decided to take a well-earned break.
Then he noticed a woman with a baby
Gazing at him with eyes so very hungry.

The waggoner was kind and good
And gave the mother half his food.
Then she asked if he could spare
A few drops of wine for her child to share.
The wagoner was compelled to decline
For he had no glass to pour the wine.

Then, from a hedge, the mother plucked
A pale, pink flower also cup-shaped,
With white stripes that, when inverted,
Served as glass for wine to be inserted !
So the wagoner filled it up to its tip
Which the mother raised to the baby's lips.

Suddenly the sun shone bright and clear
And the oxen pulled free of the mire !
The waggoner looked for the woman
But she and her baby had suddenly gone !
Yet the wagoner knew he had seen Mary
And the Lord Christ Jesus as a baby.

He drove his wagon straight into town
Where his tale soon became well-known,
Of how shared his bread and wine
With Mary and Jesus in his break-time !
And that's how it came to pass
For the pink flowers of bindweed
To be called, 'Our Lady's Little Glass'.

Wild Flowers

Among the valley's greatest powers
Must be its claim to wild flowers -
For what better reasons
For visits through the seasons:
Snowdrops or candlemas bells,
Green hellebore, bluebells as well,
The helpfulness of herb paris
And the joy of greater butterfly orchis.
But among fields of long grasses
Beware each step never trespasses
For, here, if you run or rush,
You can so easily topple and crush
Wild flowers so slender,
Precious, delightful and tender.

The Last Judgement

Fragments of Wall Mural, St Nicholas Church,
Lower Oddington

i

Down the low lane to the old church gate
Becomes a summons with Fate,
And Milton and Blake might even unite
Where the Last Judgement silently waits -
Across sacred walls it commands
Wherever you may choose to stand.

Though the figures etched in paint
Are now fragmented, faded and faint,
Sufficient remains to hold the eye
Presenting beliefs that still apply.
And what more weight can loom
Than in images depicting out Doom ?

ii

Still the mural serves to pave
The Dead rising from their graves,
Sinners becoming the Devil's slaves
Led towards Hell's fiery waves.
How it must have shook
Everyone taking their first look !

Here we are unable to avert or bury
Faith from the fourteenth century -
Where the depiction of good and evil
In Lower Oddington remains alive and well.
And where there are gaps and spaces,
Our fears insert lost faces.

And the purity of the final simplicity
Here harbours no mystery -
The Saved welcomed into their Celestial City,
While Sinners are tortured for Eternity
By monsters who gleam and glare,
And seem to dance as we stare.
But those who are good, honest and kind
The Path to Heaven shall surely find.

iv

Outside we pass a soldier's grave.
No mighty claims, no glistening symbols.
But a young man who was brave
And for whom the bell no longer tolls.
He rests from where he came
And treasured by those who know his name.
At peace in the church yard,
A corner of the Cotswolds his reward.
We lower our heads in respect
And deeper feelings begin to connect:
For, here, its more clearly seen
What a courageous life should mean -
Its purpose and fulfilment
Found glorious in the Last Judgement.

'Skimmington'

Kingham, 1912

Believing, *'with some reason',*
that her husband was 'taking away money
left to her by her father',
she shut up their house
and sent all the belongings of her husband
directly to Kingham Station,
where W. Warde Fowler,
(*Author of "A Year with 'The Birds' " etc -*
an Oxford don and leading authority on
the rare marsh warbler)
was alighting and was sufficiently impressed
to note down his observations
of happenings along the roadside line:
'of women and children and youths making
the most horrible din with old pots and pans' -
displaying their disapproval of such a wife,
who had sought refuge in a nearby cottage.

She was enduring 'Skimmington' - community action
for a wife's desertion which, at that time,
was judged a crime as much as theft.

And a wife's defence was often to be humiliated
and further burdened with the community's contempt -
as a despised neighbour and embezzled wife.

Equality and Justice and Feminism
A Trinity that, at the time,
from observations noted along that 'roadside line'
seemed further away than Heaven.

Mink Hunt

Four men lean over the bridge
to watch the lead beater
who sports a handle-bar moustache,
a bloated, yellow waistcoat,
wellingtons and a long stick
with forked-topped handle.
The beater thrashes draping branches,
strikes and slaps the river's reeds,
that are sniffed and sifted by a trailing pack of hounds.

Their coats wet, black eyes glistening, tails wagging,
as they scour and scurry over the swirling banks
crowned with meadowsweet and purple loosestrife.

The Whip is not yet twenty.
Like the mink stands out
with his yellow waistcoat,
sunglasses and gelled hair.
Clutches horn and whip.
Smiles and jokes with the men on the bridge.

The leader blows a whistle
as he scans the bramble bank,
the hounds re-appear from under the bridge
still sniffing, yelping, immersed in the hunt.
Pink-tongues and white teeth
gleam bright at the prospect of scent
sensed in the river's darkest shade.

They slurp and lurch toward Kingham,
leaving the muddied waters to settle
and the lightening return of damsel flies.

The men on the bridge join
straggling followers calling their terriers,
to share flasks of tea,
and rest on bankside logs.

The river runs quietly again, pigeons coo.
A Jack Russell terrier begs for scraps
from open-boxed packed lunches.

The sound of horns suddenly call
further up among the screen of trees and hedges.

Men and women and two young boys
grab their sticks, wave at the distant troop
gathered by the field gate.
The fork-headed, gleaming sticks strike out,
designed to pin the neck of the accursed mink.

Once more the hunters become bright-eyed,
hoping to see, spurting like a little brown torpedo,
the exposed mink
racing through swirling waters.

An hour later,
within the shadows of Bruern woods,
once more see the mink hunters
still seeking the mink,
who continues to elude and mock them,
as they make their way back down the river,
beating the bank grass,
poking the river's bushes and hedges.

Yet, unaware they, too, are being stalked,
by a pen that serves as a poet's hunting stick.

Eclipse Butterfly

11.11 a.m., 11 August, 1999

Everywhere else they stand and wait
    But I'm alone beside the largest lake,
As a cold wind comes, so much quicker,
    Causes the water to ripple and pucker,
Bends the rushes, reeds and maces.
    A shadow darkens all the green places.

I manage to see through the pin-hole
    The moon shrouding the sun's soul.
The cloudy, flickering pin-prick of light,
    Seems reluctant to convert to night -
As if begrudging a two minute contract
    Of the astronomic and historic contact.

Then the peacock butterfly circles me.
    Perhaps, the purest of winged poetry;
Disoriented by the sudden advent of night,
    Confusing this fragile symbol of sunlight.
Her colours more beautiful than anything
    This precise moment the lakes can bring.

And then it passes on with a brief breeze,
    As sunlight returns on the banks and trees.
Out of the rushes a cohort of coots emerge,
    Believing darkness has been purged.
Though the eclipse was stolen from the sky
    By the colours of a peacock butterfly.

Rough Path

I've tried to keep it until almost last,
    This long, overgrown, brambled path,
That doesn't seem to want me to pass
    As if protecting the lake for all its worth.

But now its time and I make my way
    Around nettles and high brambles,
That twist and brush to divert me away
    Where fox and badger quietly amble.

And when far behind the island cover,
    I find the hidden loop of lake territory:
Where swans and coots preen together
    As though players in some fairy-story:

Here I sense the sustenance of solitude
    Among lake and bush, hedge and tree;
Nor feel that, in some way, I also intrude
    For this scene serves different company:

A tell-tale, twisting track to a badger set;
    A startled redstart in a tangled hawthorn;
The cast-off torso from a speared trout;
    Grebes carrying debchicks newly born.

I crouch and silently watch lake activity
    Upon what is their privileged shore,
And, later, along the rough path I return,
    Keeping brambles as they were before.

Swan Lake

The great lake is like a blue tablecloth
with black spots of bobbing coots,
dipping ducks doing their rounds.
But, most of all, the fourteen swans
that are angled between banks of rushes,
or cast in mid-lake, gliding in pairs,
star-players on a bright azure table
assuming born-for roles as white, stately liners,
and the coots turning like unpredictable tugs
drawn to them like stars to the sun.

The closer I approach the more they weave
something which seems like a magic spell -
as though we know we have something to learn
from close observations of swans and not just
in the way they behave, so much more than that.
How they convey such style which, in itself,
epitomizes style - with a dignity and demeanour
that has no match, unique in their regal behaviour.
Not even the high, haughty heron can compete -
like pure silver versus twenty four carat gold.

And though the swans turn every eye,
their life-long loyalty to their chosen partner
further reveals another strength,
deeply entrenched in their characters.
More, still, the unswerving defence
of their family which they'll courageously make
against the fiercest predators - pike, fox, hawk.
Kings and Queens of Freshwaters, nature's heirs
to everything that's noble and good.
But, possibly, their only fatal flaw
when they dare to put their trust in us.

Hogweed

Holds no glamorous friends
   Only the very dubious apply:
Mayfly, alderfly, drone fly,
   Horseflies, gnats, midges
Infest the tiny white flowers:
   Feeding, seeding, breeding.
Prime bank weed of bad taste.

Give it a shake and the air
   Bristles with moody buzzing,
But all flies instantly return
   To settle on wilting flowers,
Depositing a vintage odour.
   Her trunk an ideal blow pipe.
Wonder what's birthing inside it ?

Macho Mosquitoes

Much more than they seem:
Female flying vampires,

Possess the most lethal
original syringe.

Seek, pierce, suck.
Steal their take-away meals.

Males have limited uses.
Survive on nectar, plant juices.

August Afternoon at Bourton Lakes

Sitting between long green rushes
  Near a choir that always pleases:
Courting calls of coots and geese,
  Hedgerows of robins and thrushes.

And flanking my grassy bank seat,
  High willow herbs flowering pink,
Buttercups, thistles, meadow sweet
  And butterflies' whose wings wink.

Over the gleaming, greedy grasses
  Dart the blue sticks of damselflies;
While snow-white clouds swiftly pass
  This rippling lake below blue skies.

Yet, some moments are not all fun,
  As the kingfisher suddenly dives in;
Or from soaring reeds the high heron
  Spears its beak into a flashing fin.

But lakes offer a far deeper appeal
  Where better thoughts may roam;
And, on afternoons like this, I feel
  My soul has found its dream home.

Moorhens

Near where the horse and donkey lay,
    They hazard one of their afternoon trips:
Two moorhens pick and peck their way
    Across a swathe of bankside buttercups.

But betrayed by their red crested heads
    Like bright dabs of bobbing, scarlet blood
On two black rags among grass and reeds,
    They suddenly scurry into the lake hedge.

They wait, warily emerge again, nervous
    That some hunter might be stalking them.
Then venture as far as cover of the grass,
    When one halts like some found-out victim:

Swallows swoop down and seem to tease
    The way the moorhens now hug the grass;
But the burst of a buzz-saw from the trees
    Condemns the hens back fast to their nest.

Song Thrush

For you I shall share what I know -
Of leaves soon to be gently crushed
By the early morning song thrush,
Burrowing below the high hedge-row.

At first, he does not see or hear me,
As he hops and picks, pecks and prys
For worms, grubs, seeds and flies;
But vulnerable too, off the willow tree.

His speckled breast gives him away,
Until he flutters into draping willows.
But in the gloom more brightly glows,
And his songs persuade me to stay.

And for whom would you also rush
Who could entertain in such a way,
To summon you any time of the day
Than a hostess like this song thrush ?

Dragonfly Death Dance

He'll deceive and dazzle your eyes,
as he mesmerizes and flies:

skits and skims,
turns and reverses,
dives and climbs,
and never rehearses !

If you've seen his summer routine
Its something you won't forget.

His sights soon set
on a tasty target.
Sure-fire bet
for whatever it is - he'll get !

And in half a breath,
he'll decide and deliver
a lightening fast death.

Glider and rocket,
jet and cruise bomber.
This calculating chancer
of a multi-winged dancer.

Feeding a Debchick

The sudden splash, a cry of a bird,
shielded by willow and brambles
rouses visions of some attack, but nothing
can be seen. A mid-morning mystery.

Then, between the reeds,
the great crested grebe emerges,
gliding up the river.
Its golden-brown crest glinting in the light.
But, glinting more brightly still,
the silver fish held like a vice in its beak.

The grebe moves past the island
towards her partner bringing the late breakfast
for the debchick bobbing beside her.
He juggles the fish into the debchick's beak.
But the debchick drops it. Its instantly retrieved
by the mother. She manoeuvres the fish
for a second attempt at a mid-lake exchange.
But the fish is too big for the debchick.

Mother grebe doesn't wait.
She raises fish and beak to the sky
and slips the fish down her throat.

She looks around. Satisfied with her snack.
The family move towards the bank.

The young grebe, suitably impressed,
follows obediently.
Though, now and again,
glances into the olive-green, food-rich lake.

Young Badger

Maybe some trick of light,
Until his two strips of white
Affirm I'm given first sight
Of a badger in the sunlight.

Allows me to come within
Just a few metres of him.
But looks so ragged, thin.
Heat makes his life grim.

He's young and not learnt
The fear of certain things.
And I won't teach him that
For the pleasure he brings.

Clatters onto rusty leaves
Then finds safe sanctuary,
Shaded by chestnut trees
As he scurries into old ivy.

Hunting Heron

He settles on a perfect perch -
a dead branch sticking out of the water,

serving as a survey point on which to stand,
and still within the safe haven of the island.

His grey and white colours perfect against the sky
to track fish with unerring eyes.

But when hopes fall, he goes to richer pickings,
and with a great beating of his grey wings,

rises like some primal aircraft.
Circles unsuspecting fish he'll pierce

with the precision accuracy of his beak.
He settles on the far bank for prey to seek.

Struts down to the water's edge.
His webbed feet barely raise a ripple in the water.

Then stands erect, wings enclosed.
Next to the tall willow herb. He's hard to spot.

Turns into a statue. Slim as a branch
but, from the side, he's the size of a big grey bush.

For a few minutes he hovers like that -
waiting for bank-burrowing fish to appear.

But nothing attracts his needle-sharp sight.
Once again he launches into flight,

rising from the rushes and reed and maces.
The Grey Concorde of the Lakes.

Within seconds flown away.
Highlight of an overcast, sultry river day.

Mint Leaf

She's near a minor work of art
That's too often plucked apart,
Even when she gently weaves
Those winning, unerring leaves
Among thistles and hogweeds,
We still claim her for our needs.

Though there are many others
Among this bank of wild flowers -
Harebell, thistle and rosebay,
And none should be taken away.
But in the top pocket of my shirt
The leaf of mint seals my guilt.

A Cahoot of Coots

Where ever you look they seem to be
Beside the rushes, beneath a tree,
Prowling and prying seems the norm
In search of gnat, plant or worm !

Its so easy to spot their particular type
On their beaks they bear a white stripe,
Which contrasts with shades of black
That covers them from front to back !

They float with a calm and quiet style
And circle the lake mile after mile.
You can see them anytime of the day
For they've no intention of going away.

But they often take an unexpected dip
To dusty depths that seems a trick!
Although they also like to swank a bit,
And near the swans sometimes drift.

They weave between snatching carp
And their notes can be mellow or sharp.
Yet watch out when two males go to war -
They attack each other with claws !

Its a gregarious gang most of the time,
Though some accuse them of one crime:
Never leaving a single scrap about
For coots loot whatever they scout !

Lake Thunderstorm

The lake changes its mood,
clearly instructed by the changing sky -
from blue waters and banks of shuddering green,
grey and black now invade the quivering canvas.
Ominous, war-mongering clouds
descend even lower before thunder
rumbles and reverberates over the lake.

Coot cohorts reverse direction,
hastily navigate towards bushy banks,
seeking safety in high reed ports.
The swans are already under the willow branches.

Rain sheets, triggered by thunder,
rattle and beat down, pucker
the fragile coat of the lake.
A flash of lightening illuminates the bristling lake.

Rain doubles its onslaught -
rids the lake of birds. No go zone declared.
Nothing moves or flies.
The thunderstorm rampages like a marauding viking.
Reluctant reeds cower with their green spears,
The islands seem like a misty mirage in the storm.
The rainstorm makes the lake off limits to everything.

Until the raging rain eases.
The storm rolls off eastwards.
Sunshine warily breaks out.
A few coots decide to emerge,
calling others, as they swim back out onto the lake.
Seasoned survivors of stormy battles with the sky.

A Black Swan

If white swans are the Beauties of the Lake
   Then how do we rank the black swan ?
Is she the permanent eclipse to their sun ?
   Or proof dreams hold when awake ?
If white swans are the Royals of the Lake,
   Is a black swan the reverse of things ?
What purpose does such a contrast bring ?
   Does her colour indicate freak or fake ?

A black swan will always be rare to us,
   Yet inherits a stately dignity and grace
Like her parents in whatever the place.
   Yet, they still accompany her, no less -
Making manifest their claim and their intent:
   A black swan is special but not different.

Hunting the Windrush

On the updated Ordinance Survey Map
the thin, curling blue line evaporates.

Left to tramp down muddy lanes
where horseshoe prints are traced again,
and flurries of finches
drifting between alders and hedges
affirm whose in command
of this rarely tramped tract of Windrush land.

The prospect of the marsh taken on -
skipping and sliding and slurping over
as the fabled trickle of water comes ever closer,
like the cry of gold at seeing a pool unfold.
But only drainage from the field -
the fabled pipe no where in the dry stone wall.
Even the farm is silent to a call.

Trundling down rough field paths,
past the fence where the pheasant runs;
barely edging along the steep side,
while below the infant Windrush gently glides -
fans out along the tufty valley
beneath three rough bridges the first of many.

Wild geese soar up from hideouts in the marsh,
flapping and squawking at the stranger slowly walking.

After half-a-mile,
patched-up fences block further access for a while.
Stumped on the edge of a green hollow
below winter-gripped trees fringing the horizon.
The little Windrush keeps its birthplace secret
and only the black old rooks gain daily entrance.
And, higher still, like a warning,
the muffled discharge of a shot gun.

Gull Raiding Party

Its called the bird with two hats -
the black-headed gull.
Wears funeral black in summer
But in winter their caps turn snow-white.

Up here,
a raiding party is swooping low
over an adjacent field of scattered sheep.

In precision formation
the gull platoon target the brown furrows,
unfurled by a chugging tractor.
Its bright, flashing blades
preparing a fresh brown banquet
of worms, beetles, larvae.

The gulls swoop along the furrows
as though a runway for mounting attacks.

They dip and dart, hop and strut
across the tufty fringes.
Unafraid, confident, assured.

A dangerous gathering. Their yellow beaks
fatal to anything they seek.
Strut about as if they own the field.

In winter this high land,
Birthplace of the Windrush,
claimed as their kingdom.

And teaching us, like Nature,
they're willing to completely take us back over.

‘The Sherry’

A gift for the war effort from the King of Norway,
Providing pine to build homes in ‘The Sherry’.
The black timbered frames are still reigning,
Below the tall beech trees of Temple Guiting.

Here they endure, rooted beyond their years,
As though entwined with their high tree peers;
And, maybe, imbued with that rare regal spirit,
Being a donation from a king’s restored heart.

Bales

Must be seventy at least,
white hair, thick waist,
bull-neck red as an ox.

Lifts hay bales off the jeep
and with swing of the fork
hoists them over the gate.

They land with a dull thump.
Feed for cattle.
Already heavily accelerating.

In St Mary's Churchyard, Temple Guiting

Sometimes life seems cold and hard,
But, here, sitting on a donated seat,
In St Mary's Springtime church yard,
There's no need to feel any defeat -
Among the rolling, ever greening wold
Where the Cotswold lion sheep bleat.
Nothing better could I wish to be told,
All topped by a high blackbird's song.
So close to nature eases in other ways
To bring that soothing, nourishing peace
That brightens our thoughts and our days,
Which time can neither sully or cease:
For it serves not only now but evermore
As the gentlest and safest of armour.

Tumbling from Temple Guiting

Surpassing all tests and trials
on a journey that stretches for miles.

Tumbles and bubbles,
ripples and races.

Flows through slanting hills,
cruises between banks and rills.

Chuckles and chivvies,
twists and turns.

Babbles in the morning haze
where cattle and sheep graze.

Splashes and crashes,
Dawdles and dashes.

Even when lost from sight,
Sparkles in the moonlight.

Swirls and curls,
Lingers and loiters.

Never likes to stay,
Simply loves to run far away.

Sometimes struggles,
Gurgles and guggles.

Sweeps past field, farm, gate.
Winding Windrush won't wait !

High Choir

Up here there's an unmapped border,
Where the branches of a storm-laid alder
Offers a solitary seat
To hear February's heart-beat:

The Windrush carves a curving course,
Finds the neighing of a distant horse.
And the music from a chorus of birds,
Who need no lyrics or words.

Shrouded within woodland and thicket
Other feelings slowly felt:
Burgeoning with buds before sunlight.
Filtering through, crisp and bright.

And no track leaves a trace
How to find this high, untouched place
That has been kept so rare.
Its seems far too good to ever share -

Alders and willows and firs and hawthorns
Serve as resident guardians;
While dandelions and clusters of snowdrops
Provide the current crops.

Where this high choir reigns
A little longer I shall remain,
Gathering a few moments to take away
And visit again on darker days.

Clapper Bridge

Here it feels good to be alone
Standing on the fording bridge of stone.
Hard and worn from aeons of tread.
Now subject to clinging lichen on the river bed.

How smooth the stone against the hand.
What stories it could tell about this land !
The river has carved the curves in the stone
Which gleams with the texture of bone.

Pebbles and stones sparkle on the river floor
As clear as gems in a jewel store.
Though other things keep dreams in check -
An orange cartridge case, a jeep tyre track.

This is working and hunting territory
With little time for rhyme or fantasy.
But astride on the clapper bridge of stone
Feel the pleasure of being alone and not alone.

Morning Hunt

A lost hound runs and rummages
    Along the ploughed field's thorn hedge.
Seeking the scent he knows will place
    Him right back in the morning race.

A huntsmen holds up the tracking cars.
    His whip directs where the action spurs
And there the stragglers eagerly proceed,
    Rocking back and for on their steeds.

Courteous nods and swift 'Thank You's !'
    Ring out above clattering horse shoes,
Pursued by another pack of followers
    In their tweeds and dangling binoculars,

Trailing the straddling, scarlet coats
    Weaving between beeches and oaks;
As the sound of the hounds high cries
    Rise from where the Windrush hides -

Below the thickets of alders and firs
    The scarlet coats begin to blur,
Where the hounds must be entirely left
    To seize or lose the quarry of the hunt,

Who seems to imitate the river itself,
    As if inspired by the thought of death -
Scours and swerves, dips and runs
    Then flashes famously out in the sun !

Snowdrop Bank

Deposited in the heart of a Barton bank
Now grown to quite a considerable sum,
Causing its investors to annually blink
When profits are presented to them.
Even when winter markets are bleak
They can be part of the portfolio to trust
To bolster the darkest January week.
And that's why investors like them best.
Once seeded they can be left to grow
And won't tumble or falter before the frost,
Or cower and collapse below a fall of snow.
After Xmas they issue maximum interest:
First flowers the New Year account brings
And guarantee the growing riches of Spring.

Navigating Naunton

There's no point being down there on the ground.
You won't see anything.
Too many gates, fences, hedges, walls, sheds,
posts, greenhouses, bushes.
No public path for the rambler.
Just as well. Keeps the Windrush unspoiled.

Here's the best view:
On the high road towards Stow.
Stand here and you'll see Naunton
stretched out like a grey ribbon - stone buildings
along the foot of green and brown fields banking up
towards rims of hawthorns, ashes and firs and oaks.

Naunton lies spread out as if on a map.
Ideal for navigating the journey of the Windrush,
where it emerges in the west among a cluster of stone roofs.

The sight of headstones stretched out
looks awesome from here:
Puts everything into perspective -
and you begin to think whether tracking a river
is worthy enough reason for a serious living.
But a serious thing, in fact, may just be tracking a river
through the course of a village where danger is measured
by the height of water against a post.

Small things reveal the real life of a village.
A woman appears from a garden shed
cradling a baby in a white blanket.
A collie dog runs around her. Desperate to play.
Three ducks scuttle onto the grass near the bridge.
Little activities break the mould of stone
and occasional patches of turned, waiting earth.

The mother is joined by another woman
walking her dog, a retriever.
They pause to talk at the third and last bridge.

One is wood and leads to a playground.
Another is made of odd planks, branches.
At the eastern end, there's a small, sturdy stone bridge.
Though many more screened by firs and stone walls.

From here it seems the river is calm
and quiet through all the seasons -
and the greenery along this side of the bank
looks safe and spacious for children.

In 1779 Naunton was reputed to be 'the healthiest place
in all England with a death rate of only one percent'.

No wonder people tried to navigate their lives
to settle with their families down there
in that small, river-running village
nestling in the cusp of a green, tree-topped valley.

Even now, early in the morning or late in the evening,
they are free to seek the company of the Windrush,
still threading its way through the village -

discreet, unaffected and still serving
as a constant, comforting, consoling companion.

The River Windrush

Descending from high to low wolds
The Windrush seizes all its chances.
Nor needs an explanation with words
To awaken dormant, rusted senses.

Its never to late to visit her show
With her winding and winning way -
To wood, field, bank and meadow
For delights that appear every day.

When the Windrush waves her wand
She makes strangers her friends,
As she flows through Cotswold land
Offering company that never ends.

Christmas Eve in a Cotswold Barn

High on the farm over the hill
    Trees and hedges sway;
Where the wind cold and shrill,
    Keeps a white xmas at bay.

All evening the tempest growls,
    Loses its temper everywhere:
Rattles and lashes at windows,
    Behaves like a bolting mare.

The barn becomes a galleon,
    Anchored in a spitting sea;
Stands fast fighting alone,
    Battling the barracking bully.

In the midst of the howling night
    The farmer clutches his stick,
And casts his white flashlight
    Across his undercover flock.

In the barn, safe and warm,
    Remain his shuttered sheep,
Haboured from raging harm.
    Even the lambs are asleep.

Though the gale rages outside,
    The barn fends off all fear.
A haven it will always provide
    Like Bethlehem drawing near.

Resources

Adlestrop Footpaths Committee	Historical Notes and Drawings of the Four Circular Walks in Adlestrop and Daylesford
Adlard, Eleanor	Winchcombe Cavalcade
Beckworth, E.G.C.	On the Hill
Briggs, Katharine M.	The Folklore of the Cotswolds
Brill, Edith	Life and Traditions in the Cotswolds
Brill, Edith	Old Cotswold
Brill, Edith	Portrait of the Cotswolds
Butler, Burt	A Cotswold Ragbag
Clifford, Harry	A History of Bourton on the Water
Coldicott, F.W.	Memories of an Old Campdonian
Day, David	The Duck Pond Affair Etc
Dee, Joanna E.	Bibury
Delderfield, Eric R.	The Cotswolds Countryside and its Characters
Donaldson, D.N.	A Portrait of Winchcombe
Feachem, Dr. W. R.	History of St. Mary's Church, Temple Guiting
Fees, Craig (Editor)	A Child in Arcadia
Gordon, Catherine	Chipping Campden
Gurney, Ivor	Collected Poems
Hadfield, C. and M.	The Cotswolds
Harris, Mollie	Where The Windrush Flows
Hill, Susan	The Spirit of the Cotswolds
Horne, John	Chipping Campden from the Grass Roots
Houghton, C.C.	A Walk About Broadway
Hudson, John	A Year in the Cotswolds
Jelly, Molly	Butchers, Billets and Buses
Jelly Molly	Growing Up in Moreton Between the Wars
Johnson, Joan	A Short History of Moreton in Marsh
Kibble, John	Charming Charlbury
Lewis, June R.	Cotswold Villages
Massingham, H. J.	Cotswold Country
Massingham, H. J.	Wold Without End
Meades, Eileen	A History of Chipping Norton
Meadows, Catherine	'The City of Dorn' in Memories of Moreton
Moreton in Marsh Local History Society	Memories of Moreton
Moriarty, Denis	Buildings of the Cotswolds
Nelson, J. P.	Broad Campden, a supplement

Oakey, John	Reminiscences of Winchcombe
Powell, Geoffrey	The Book of Campden
Rushen, Percy	A History of Chipping Campden
Rushen, Percy	Handbook to Chipping Campden
Thomas, Edward	Selected Poems
Turner, Mark	Folklore and Mysteries of the Cotswolds
Viner, David	The North Cotswolds in Old Photographs
Warde Fowler, W.	Kingham Old and New
Warren, C. Henry	A Cotswold Year
Whitfield, Christopher	A History of Chipping Campden
Wilson MacArthur	The River Windrush
W. I. of Guiting Power	Guiting Power and Farmcote
Wray, T. & Stratford, D.	Bourton on the Water
Wright, L. & Priddey, J.	Cotswold Heritage

~~~~~~~~~~~~~~~~~~~~~~~~

~~~~~~~~~~~~~~~~~

~~~~~~~~~
~~~~~~~~~